Governor in Manipur State Politics

About the Author

Dr. Karam Kunjani Devi is the daughter of (L) K. Tonjao Singh and Karam (O) (L) Amubi Devi of Kyamgei Mamang Leikai. She has two sisters and two brothers. She got her B.A. Political Science Honours from Manipur College, Imphal in 1974, and became an M.A. in Political Science in 1976 from JNU Centre, Canchipur. She got her Ph.D under the supervision of Prof. Ksh. Bimola Devi, Former Dean School of Social Sciences, Manipur University, with the title of *"Role of Governor in the State Politics of India, with Special Reference to Manipur"*, in 1991. She had contributed eight articles in books and journals (National and International). She had attended and presented papers in seminars, conferences, symposias, talk programmes at State, national and international levels. She was working as Reader, Associate Professor and Head of Political Science at Lilong Haoreibi College, Lilong for many years and recognized Ph.D Supervisor in the Department of Political Science, Manipur University. At present she is working as Principal in-charge of Lilong Haoreibi College, Lilong.

Governor in Manipur State Politics

Karam Kunjani Devi

CONCEPT PUBLISHING COMPANY PVT. LTD.
NEW DELHI-110059

ISBN-13: 978-93-5125-045-6

First Published 2015

Published and Printed by

Concept Publishing Company Pvt. Ltd.
A/15-16, Commercial Block, Mohan Garden
New Delhi-110059 (India)
T: 25351460, 25351794, *F*: 091-11-25357109
E: publishing@conceptpub.com, W: www.conceptpub.com
Editorial Office: H-13, Bali Nagar, New Delhi-110 015, India.

Cataloging in Publication Data—*Courtesy:* D.K. Agencies (P) Ltd. <docinfo@dkagencies.com>

Kunjani Devi, Karam , author.
Governor in Manipur State politics / Karam Kunjani Devi.
pages ; cm
Includes bibliographical references (pages) and index.
ISBN 9789351250715

1. Governors—India—Manipur. 2. Manipur (India)—Politics and government—20th century. I. Title.

DDC 352.23213095417 23

Dedication

Dedicated to my father

(L) Karam Tonjao Singh

without whose care and support my life
should not take this present shape.

Foreword

The role of the Governor and a State of India federation has become very important and critical since the middle of 1960s. The importance was not felt so much in the 1950s and the first half of 1960s. During this one and a half decade, the Indian National Congress was the ruling party at both the national as well as in the States of India except Kerala in 1957. Moreover, the national government and the administration in the States was under the guidance of the towering personality of Jawaharlal Nehru as Prime Minister of India. The death of Jawaharlal Nehru in 1964 and the emergence of non-Congress governments in some States of India after the general elections in 1967 had resulted in the changing role of the Governor in matters relating to the State politics as well as in the administrative. In the earlier phase, the Governor was only the nominal head of State where the real political and administrative powers lie in the hands of the Chief Minister of the State. As the Governor has been appointed by the President of India, he is responsible and accountable to the President. But in reality it is the Council of Ministers, particularly the Prime Minister who exercise informal control and guidance to the Governor.

When the appointment of the Governor was discussed in the Constituent Assembly, there were three proposals. The first was that the Governor should be directly elected by the people on the basis of adult franchise. Second, the Governor should be appointed by the President from a panel of four candidates to be elected by the members of the State legislature in accordance with the system of proportional representation by means of a single transferable vote. And third he should be directly appointed by the President. After a thorough discussion, the first proposal was rejected on the ground that the direct election of the Governor by the people will had to friction with the Chief Minister. And the second will create a lot of resentment in the State Legislature if the person in the top of the panel is not appointed and the appointed person would be a party man, a nominee of the Chief Minister. The third proposal was accepted by the members of the Constituent Assembly. Thus the Governor is the connecting link between the national government and the State government.

This dual role of the Governor may sometimes lead by conflict of loyalties. This particularly happens when the State Ministry belongs to a party other than the party which is in power at the Centre.

The Constitution of India had given legislative, executive, judicial, financial, power to promulgate Ordinance and the emergency powers to be exercised under Article 356 of the Constitution of India.

In exercising legislative power, the Governor may reserve a bill for the consideration of the President of India. When no party enjoys majority after the Assembly elections, the Governor has the option of inviting the single largest party or any coalition of political parties to form the government, No money bill can be introduced in the Legislative Assembly except on the recommendation of the Governor. The Governor is not merely the head of a State, a figurehead or a rubber stamp he is an essential part of the constitutional machinery of parliamentary democracy.

Manipur had attained the status of full fledged statehood on 21st January 1972. The Governor of Assam was also the Governor of Manipur. As no political party secured majority to form government after the Assembly elections 1972, 1974, 1980, 1985, 1990, 1995 and 2002, The Governor of Manipur had played his role very carefully in inviting the leader of the coalition of political parties headed by national political party and regional political party to form government. It was only after the Assembly elections

2007 and 2012 that the Governor had invited the leader of the Congress party which secured majority to form the government without facing coalition politics.

Dr. K. Kunjani Devi, in her present book, *Governor in Manipur State Politics* examines the role of the Governor in the politics, Manipur since 1972-90. She has selected important areas for her study like Governor and the Legislature, Governor and Council of Ministers, Governor and Discretionary Governor and Centre-State relations, Special Powers of the Governors in Hill Areas of Manipur, etc. The information and findings of her research work will ultimately help one to understand the role of the Governor in the different stages of the political process of Manipur. The work is a new contribution to the available literature of the politics of Manipur.

I wish Dr. K. Kunjani Devi a grand success in her academic pursuits and future academic life by publishing such valuable books in the area of her choice.

Ksh. Bimola Devi
Former Dean,
School of Social Sciences
Manipur University

Preface

The institution of the Governor has become very important in the federal politics of India. There are many controversies regarding the role of the Governors in the State politics of India, especially after 1967. For examining the Centre-State relations in India, one cannot also ignore the powers, functions and the role of the Governor in the State, since it has become, if not always, a subject of controversy in recent years. There are published literatures on the Governor in General and case study of particular State in India. But so far, I believe, there is no proper and clear work of the Governor of the State of Manipur. The object of the study, therefore, is to examine the role of the Governor in Manipur and at the same time examine the constitutional provisions and the practices followed in other States of India.

The first chapter is the introduction. It deals with the historical background of the institution of Governor in a general way. So we need to have a good research work in connection with the study of the institution of Governor of each and every State of India for understanding about the clear structure of the Indian federalism. The second chapter examines the role of the Governor as the head of the State, the role of the Governor changes according to the political changes at the Centre. When the Centre and States are ruled by the same political party his role is good and calm but becomes crucial when different political parties rule at the Centre and the State. Chapter three studies the relationship between the Governor and the Legislature which points out the exact role of a legislative head of the State. The relationship between the Governor and the Council of Ministers which is very important in the present day politics of the State, is discussed in chapter four.

Chapter five again takes up the controversial issue of discretionary powers of the Governor in Manipur from 1972-1988 different Governors exercise discretionary powers in appointing Chief Ministers, dismissing Ministry, dissolving Legislative Assemblies and imposing President's Rule very frequently due to political instability in the State. Special Powers of the Governors of Assam Meghalaya, Tripura and Mizoram under the Sixth Schedule of the Constitution of India are minutely discussed here. For example, under clause 1(3) of the Schedule the Governor has the power to include, exclude and diminish the area of any State. He can also alter the name of any autonomous district and define its boundaries. Manipur is not under the Sixth Schedule of the Constitution of India. So the Governor of Manipur has no power under this Schedule. But Constitution of India under Article 371(C) provides the Governor of Manipur certain discretionary power and respectively for hill areas. In short the Governor is involved in all the aspects of State developments.

The role of the Governor in Centre-State relations, which is the burning issue of Indian politics today is discussed separately in chapter six. The last chapter tries to study in brief the role of the Governor in General and makes suggestions for more important parts. The Governor has to play more and more meaningful roles so that the States in India including Manipur can achieve climax of development in the federal politics of India.

I take this opportunity to offer my grateful thanks to my teacher, wellwisher, and Ph.D. supervisor, Prof. Ksh. Bimola Devi, former Dean, School of Social Sciences, Manipur University, who advises me to work on these lines, and giving the Forwarding Note for this volume.

Next, I owe my profound debt to Concept Publishing Company Pvt. Ltd. for their kind acceptance for publishing this volume into a book form.

Again, I owe my sincere thanks to my friends—Binarani, Urmila, Muhindro and others who inspired and helped me to articulate my ideas in developing this volume.

I also thank my sister K. Momon Devi, and my friend, M. Indumukhi Devi, Assistant Librarian, Manipur State Legislative Assembly Library, who helped me a lot in the collection of materials.

27th December, 2013 **K. Kunjani Devi**

Contents

Abbreviations

C.C.P.A.	Central Committee for Parliamentary Affairs.
Cong.(I)	Indira Congress.
Cong.(O)	Congress Organisation.
C.P.I.	Communist Party of India
C.P.I.(M)	Communist Party of India (Marxist)
D.M.K.	Dravidra Munnetra Kazaghum.
D.L.P	Democratic Legislative Party
K.N.A.	Kuki National Assembly.
M.H.U.	Manipur Hill Union.
M.L.A.	Member of Legislative Assembly
M.P.	Member of Parliament.
M.P.P.	Manipur People's Party
N.P.P.	National People's Party
P.D.F.	Progressive Democratic Front.
P.I.G	Progressive Independent Group.
P.W.D.	Public Works Department.
Retd.	Retired
S.S.P.	Sanyukta Socialist Party.
S.V.D.	Sanyukta Vidhayak Dal.
U.L.P.	United Legislative Party.
U.S.A.	United States of America.
U.S.S.R.	Union of Socialist Soviet Russia.

CHAPTER-I

Introduction

The office of the Governor has become very important in a federal country like India. The executive power of the Indian States is vested in the Governor as the executive power of the Union vests in the Resident and all the executive action of the State has to be taken in the name of the Governor. Normally there is a Governor for each State but it is possible to appoint the same person as Governor for two or more States. He exercises his executive power either directly or through his subordinates. The study of power, functions and role of the Governor forms a major section in analyzing the whole political system theoretically and practically.

Encyclopaedia Britannica defines, "Governor as a common political title for the official head of a dependent or component unit in a larger constitutional structure".[1]

No constitution in the world has been able to divorce itself completely from the past. Here we can mention the words of Jennings—"All constitutions are the heirs of the past as well as the testator of the future".[2]

Historical Background

Let us trace the institution of Governorship in India chronologically starting from the Hindu period.

Hindu Period: During the time of Chandragupta (321-300 B.C.), the Maurya empire was divided into four provinces. "The officers of the provinces were designated as Kumars. They were the heads of the provinces and sometimes some Mahamantras were seen along with the Kumars".[3] The Kumaras and Mahamantras were the Governor and Deputy Governors respectively.

During the time of Ashoka (273-232 B.C.) "The Rajukas were in the highest position and were sometimes governors of provinces. The Purushas carried out the wishes of the king and kept liaison between the king and the Rajukas. In the Ashokan era, it is known that next to the Emperor, the Governor played a significant role having different subordinates in carrying out the administration of the province.

Muslim Period: During the reign of Akbar (1556-1605) "each Suba (Province) was governed by a Sipah Salar (Governor) popularly known as Subedar. He had almost unlimited authority over the civil and military affairs".[4] In the concerned provinces, the Governor possessed supreme power. When Shahjahan (1627-1658) was the Mughal Emperor, the appointment of the Governor was really made by the Emperor himself from his royal family particularly from among his sons. "In 1645, while Aurangzeb was Governor of Gujarat he converted the temple of Chintaman into a mosque and named it Quwatul-Islam".[5] This shows the supreme power of the Governor in the administration of the province.

"From March 1648 to July 1652, Aurangzeb was Governor of Multan and Sindh....".[6] Again, Murad, Governor of Gujarat, the youngest of Shahjahan's sons was courageous and brave but he had no control over his tongue and temper. He had been appointed Governor of Bengal and Orissa".[7]

Aurangzeb appointed the Governors from his officials according to their calibre. "In the year 1660, Mirjumle, the lieutenant of Aurangzeb, was appointed Governor of Bengal"[8]; and "ordered to punish lawless zamindars of the province, especially those of Assam and Magh (Arrakan)".[9]

The Timur rulers also appointed the Governors from their near and dear ones. During the ruler of Jahangir Shah (1712-1713), the first son of Bahadur Shah, Azimush Shah, "was Governor of Bengal, Bihar and Orissa".[10] There was also instance of common

Governorship. From such Governorship it seems that the personality of the concerned person played a great role in running the administration of two or more units or provinces. Moreover, there was also, simultaneously, separate institution of Deputy Governor. Under the rule of Farukh-Siyar (1707-1719) another Mughal counterpart of Bahadur Shah, one "Saf Shikan Khan was the Deputy Governor of Orissa,"[11] and "Nasir Khan the Deputy Governor of Kabul who had accumulated great wealth".[12] The main function of the Deputy Governor was to collect revenue or any other source of finance from the province.

During the reign of Farukh-Siyar the Governor also tried at their best level to keep close relationship with the Britishers who came to India as traders. "A notable event of Farukh-Siyar's reign was the grant of valuable trade concessions and exemptions from customs duties to the East India Company which had sent from Calcutta to protest against the exactions of the Bengal Governor".[13]

From the above discussion we know that the institution of the Governor in India was not the outcome of the Britishers. It was existed before the arrival of the British imperialism in the country.

"The Origin of the office of the Governor came into existence when the Queen Elizabeth (1558-1603) granted the trading powers to the company of Merchants of London into the East Indies under the famous Charter of 31st December 1600".[14]

The British policy of sending the group of traders to India for the first time was not meant only for business sake but also for dominating politically the whole India. "The Control of the company's business was invested in a Governor and the twentyfour committees".[15] The company was headed by the Governor with a clear political commitment.

"According to the Charter of 1600, the executive power of the company were vested in the Governor".[16] The power management and the control of the affairs of the company were under the responsibility of the Governor. He was also to promote the interest of the company. Some specified legislative and judicial powers were also granted to him to safeguard the interest of the company. "The Governor was empowered to impose fines or penalties as were necessary to enforce the laws against offenders".[17] In these quotations it is seen that the Governors play all the three legislative, executive and judiciary roles and also behave like to chief of the State.

After Seventeenth century, the office of the Governor became very important and more and more powers were vested in the Governor for consolidating the interest of the British Rule in India.

"The Charter Act of 1661 further empowered the Governor with civil and criminal powers to safeguard the interest of the company".[18] Though the Governor was to function under the control and supervision of the general court in London he practically exercised all the powers and privileges which were granted by the British Crown to the Company. "The powers exercised by the Governor were not sufficient to protect the commercial and trading interest of the East India Company, especially owing to the gradual disintegration of Mughal Empire after the death of Aurangzeb and secondly owing to the rivalry and conflict of French and Portuguese trading companies in India".[19] These factors led the British to divert the intention of the Company from commercial interest to territorial and political gains for consolidating the position of the company in India.

In short, the attempt to control the tiny Mughal kingdom, and desire to supersede the trading interest of both the French and the Portuguese trader in India are the main causes which quickens the British Government to introduce the institution of Governor in India. Different scholars are giving different statements in connection with the power and position of Governor in India with the arrival of the British East India Company. "Consequently, the governor was further given the powers of civil and military administration".[20]

"The Charter of 1669 authorized the Governor to exercise all those powers intended for any Captain/General of the Army by virtue of his office".[21]

"The Charter of 1677 and 1683 entrusted the Governor with more powers especially the power to declare war and to make peace.

"Under the Charter Act of 1698 each Presidency of the Company was brought under the control of the governor and council appointed by the commission of the Company".[22]

In short, the administration of each presidency was vested in a Governor and a council consisting of senior servants of the company. Both the Governor and the council jointly exercise their powers. Thus the British Crown had gradually increased the power of the Governor through series of Acts.

In 1773, the British Parliament, in order to consolidate the authority of the Company in India, enacted "The East India Company Act, 1773 which is generally known as Regulating Act".[23] The Act introduced the policy of centralization in three presidencies, viz., Bengal, Bombay and Madras. The Presidency of Bengal was ruled by a Governor General while that of Bombay and Madras were headed by a Governor. Under the clause 9 of this Regulating Act the Governors of Bombay and Madras presidencies were under the supervision and control of the Governor General of Bengal. Thus "the Act limited the independent role of the Governors of Bombay and Madras"[24] which become to some extent the agencies of the Governor General-in-Council of India.

Under the Act of 1859, "the first phase of the Company's role in India came to an end and India was to be governed by and in the name of Her Majesty".[25] Regarding the provincial Government the Act mentioned that the appointment of the Governors "shall be made by Her Majesty by warrant under her Royal sign Manual".[26] But no change was made in the powers and functions of the Governor.

The Indian Council Act of 1909 which is known as Morely-Minto-Reforms empowered the Governor of each presidency "to appoint a member of the provincial council as vice-president for the purpose of holding and executing the office of the Governor temporarily or for presiding over the meeting in the absence of the Governor".[27]

Under the Government of India Act 1919, the Governors of the British provinces of Bengal, Madras and Bombay were continued to be appointed by British Crown for a period of 5 years while in other provinces the Governors were to be appointed under the "seal of the Crown after consultation with the Governor-General".[28] The Governor also could appoint a Minister of the Legislative Council within a period of six months".[29]

In August 1935, the British Government introduced the Government of India Act 1935 which is also known as provincial Autonomy Act. Under this Act "the whole executive authority of a Province was vested in the Governor".[30] In exercising the executive power of the province the Governor has to play three different roles". (1) In some cases he was to act in his discretion. There was no need for him to consult his Ministers; (2) In some cases he was to act in his individual judgment where he might consult his Ministers but was not bound by their advice; and (3) He was to act on the advice of the Council of Ministers".[31]

In the field of legislation also "he was empowered to make rules for the more convenient transaction of the business of the provincial government".[32] "He could summon, prorogue and dissolve the provincial Legislature in his discretion. He could address or send messages to it and could call a joint sitting if there were two chambers".[33] Moreover, "no bill passed by the Legislative Council could become the law of the Province without the consent of the Governor. He could give his assent to a Bill, withhold it, or return it for reconsideration, or reserve it for the sanction of the Governor-General".[34]

The Government of India Act 1935, also provides that "if at any time when the Provincial Legislature was not in session and that if Governor was satisfied that circumstance exists which rendered it necessary for him to take immediate action, he might promulgate an ordinance in his name. This ordinance was to be approved by the Legislature and it had the same force and effect as an Act of the Provincial Legislature assented to by the Governor".[35] "The Governor also had the power to issue proclamation in his discretion if he was satisfied that a situation had arisen in which the government of the province could not be carried on in accordance with the provisions of the Act of 1935".[36]

Thus from the Government of India Act 1935, we know that the Central Government had delegated in the hands of Governor the administrative authority of the province. The governor became an absolute constitutional head (dictator) of the Province because of the discretionary power and special responsibilities given by the Central Government. In short, under this Act the Governor was the real ruler of the provincial administration during the British period. Moreover, in the election of the Legislative Councils (Upper Chamber). The concerned Governor had the power to be "filled by nomination ten seats in Madras, eight in Bengal and the United Provinces and four in the other provinces".[37]

Comparative Analysis

A comparative analysis can be made of the Governors of the three different periods—Hindu, Muslim and the British. During the Hindu period, the Governors were the heads of the provinces and in running the administration of the respective province they had many subordinates.

In the Muslim period, the Governors had almost unlimited authority over the civil and military affairs of the concerned province. The Emperors appointed the Governors on the calibre basis.

During the British period, the powers and functions of the Governor increased from time to time and step by step and ultimately the Governors became the real rulers of the provinces. But they had to enjoy the confidence of the British Crown.

The Governors during the British period had enjoyed more powers and function then the Governor of the Hindu period and Muslim period. The reason is that the Hindu and Muslim kings had entrusted limited powers and functions to the Provincial heads while the British ruler provided more and more autonomy from time to time to the provincial agents, i.e.. the Governors.

Governor in Other Federal States

Governors are the heads of the federating units of the two leading federal countries in the world—the USA and the USSR.

The American Constitution does not mention the Governorship but the state executive is headed by the Governor. The Chief executive of the American state was originally elected and controlled by the state legislature. He had acquired practical independence through successive constitutional revisions.

The Soviet Constitution of 1977 under Art. 128 states that the Council of Ministers of the USSR is the highest executive and administrative body of the state authority of the USSR. The Council of Ministers of the USSR is formed by the Supreme Soviet of USSR at joint sitting of the Soviet of Union and the Soviet of Nationalities and consist of the Chairman of the Council of Ministers of the USSR, and Chairman of the state Committees of the USSR.

The Chairman of the Council of Ministers of the Union Republics shall be ex-officio members of the Council of Ministers of the USSR.

INDIA

The Britishers left India in 1947. It became a Republic in 1950 with its own Constitution which contained all the necessary structures of an independent country.

Like the Government of India Act 1935, the Constitution of India of 1950 provides for a federal form of Government. The State administration is headed by a Governor appointed by the President for a period of 5 years. Article 153 of the Constitution of India states that there shall be a Governor for each State. Again, Article 155 provides that the Governor of a State shall be appointed by the President by warrant under his hand and seal. In the Parliamentary context, the Governor is to be aided and advised by the Council of Ministers and so long as the Ministry enjoys the confidence of the State Legislature the Governor dares no interference. As the Governor of the Central Government he has to play a dual role:

(i) To advise the State Ministry on various important political and administrative issues and

(ii) To keep the Central government informed about the working of the constitutional machinery of the State. This dual role of the Governor can sometimes lead to a conflict that particularly happens when State Ministry belongs to a party other than the party which is in power at the Centre.

MANIPUR

Manipur merged the Indian Union on 15th October, 1949. With the application of the Merger States (Laws) Act 1949, the administration of Manipur was taken over by a Chief Commissioner and remained as a Part C State under the Constitution of India. The former Council of Ministers and the Legislative Assembly were dissolved. The Maharaja was no longer the head of the State (under the Manipur State Constitution Act 1947). In his place, the Chief Commissioner became the head of the State.

In response to the popular demand for responsible Government Article 239A was inserted to the Constitution of India, granting a Legislative Assembly to Manipur. Accordingly the Government of Union Territories Act 1963 was enacted by parliament. According to this Act, the head of the State was known as Administrator, though usually known as Chief Commissioner of Manipur.

Manipur has got statehood on the 21st January 1972 under the North-Eastern Areas (Reorganisation) Act 1971. At that time, Manipur was headed by a common Governor. The Governor of Manipur was also the Governor of Assam, Meghalaya, Nagaland and Tripura. In accordance with Article 153 of the Constitution of India, the administration of Manipur is headed by a Governor. Like the Governor of other States, the Governor of Manipur is appointed by the President and he usually holds office for a period of 5 years.

It may be said that the Governor of the North-Eastern Region of India was a super Governor having a high status for maintaining law and order in the hilly region having bad communication system. Really the power and functions of the Governor in Manipur was far more than the Governors of other Indian States. Constitutional Amendments of the Constitution of India also provides for special powers to the Governor of Manipur. For example, Article 371C(2) of the Constitution of India lays down that the Governor shall annually, or whenever required by the President, make a report to the President regarding the administration of the Hill Areas in the State of Manipur and the executive power of the Union shall extend to the giving of directions to the State as to the administration of the said areas. Since 1981, the Governor of Manipur was the Governor of Nagaland and Tripura only. Again, from 10th July 1989, Manipur has a separate Governor of her own.

In the working of the Indian federation, the institution of Governor cannot be neglected. Its importance has increased day by day due to various political issues like the demand of autonomy by the States, growth of regional political parties, etc. The nature of the Indian federation is also another factor, giving importance to the role of the Governor of a State.

The role of the Governor in the working of the Indian political system is even more important in a small State like Manipur. Very often the politics of Manipur is characterized by political instability. The stability and instability of the Ministry sometimes depends upon the role of the Governor.

An attempt has been made in the following chapters to examine the role of the Governor in Indian politics at large and in Manipur in particular.

References

1. *Encyclopaedia Britannica,* Vol. 10, Encyclopedia Britanica, Inc. William Benton Publishers, U.S.A., 1971, p. 640.
2. Shukala, V.N., '*The Constitution of India*', Eastern Book Company, Lucknow, 1975, 6th Edn., Reprint 1981, Introduction, p. XI-14.
3. Bhattacharjee Arun, '*History of Ancient India*', Sterling Publisher, New Delhi, 1979, 1st Edn., p. 174.
4. Khanna and Chopra, *India Ancient and Mediaeval,* The Macmillan Co. of India Ltd., 1976, p. 230.
5. S.R. Sharma, '*Mughal Empire in India*', Lashim Narain Agarwal Educational Publishers, Agra-3, 1979, 8th Edn., p. 277.
6. *Ibid.*, p. 271.

7. Khanna and Chopra, *op. cit.,* p. 254.
8. S.R. Sharma, *op. cit.,* p. 273.
9. Sarkar Jadurnath, '*History of Aurangzeb*', Vol. I, Orient Longman Ltd. New Delhi, 1972, p. 124.
10. S.R. Sharma, *op. cit.*, p. 373.
11. *Ibid.,* p. 376.
12. *Ibid.*, p. 377.
13. Khanna and Chopra, *op. cit.*, p. 275.
14. Saharay, H.K., '*A Legal Study of Constitutional Development of India*', Nabha Ral Publishers, Calcutta, 1970, pp. 35-36.
15. Banerjee, Anil Chandra, (Ed), '*Indian Constitutional Documents*', Vol. I, A Mukherjee Private Co. Ltd., Calcutta, 1948, p. XIII.
16. Mukherji, Panchananda, (Ed), *Indian Constitutional Documents*, Thacker Spin & Co., Calcutta, 1980, 2nd Edn., pp. XII-XIV.
17. *Ibid.*, p. XIV.
18. Sikri, S.L., '*The Constitutional History of India*', Vol. I, S. Nagin & Co., Jullundar, 1964, 3rd Edn., p. 5.
19. Thompson, Edward & Garrot, G.T., '*Rise and Fulfilment of British Rule in India*', Central Book Depot, Allahabad, 1969, pp. 19-20.
20. Mukherjee, Panchananda, *op. cit.,* p. XVII.
21. Banerjee A.C., *op. cit.,* p. XIV.
22. Saharay, R.K., *op. cit.,* pp. 37-38.
23. Keith, A.B., '*A Constitutional History of India*', Central Book Depot, Allahabad, 1961, 2nd Edn., p. 70.
24. Banerjee A.C., *op. cit.*, p. 21.
25. Singh G.N., *Landmarks in India: Constitutional and Development.* Vol. I, Ahua Ram & Sons, Delhi, 1952, 3rd Edn., p. 65.
26. Under the clause 29 of the Act the Governor General of India could appoint the Act the Governor General of India could appoint the Lieutenant Governor of a Province subject to an approbation of Her Majesty.
27. Banerjee, A.C., *op. cit.*, p. 235.
28. *Ibid.*, p. 34.
29. *Ibid.*, p. 35.
30. *Ibid.*, p. 279.
31. Sikri, S.L.. *op. cit.*, p. 179.
32. Banerjee, A.C., *op. cit.*, p. 284.
33. Keith, A.B., *op. cit.*, p. 352.
34. Keith, A.B., *op. cit.*, pp. 354-355.
35. Banerjee, A.C., *op. cit.*, pp. 286-287.
36. *Ibid.*, pp. 289-290.
37. V.N. Shukla, The Constitution of India, *op. cit.*, p. XIV.

CHAPTER-II

The Governor as Head of the State

Historical Background

Governor as head of the State is important in a federation because the head of the whole country or the Central Government alone is not able to run the administration of the country very smoothly. Every head of the State is required to keep sub-heads under him as his representatives in administrative affairs of the concerned units or States. The administrative efficiency of a federal State is really depended upon the efficient service of the Governors.

The origin of the institution of the Governor is not a recent one. It has a long history in the world context. Even in India, the institution can be traced back to early Hindu period. The Governors in the different phases of history has acted as the administrative agent of the Emperors who had delegated to them some of his administrative powers. The Governors who were appointed and removed by the Emperor paid tributes and homages to the Emperors from time to time.

During the British Rule, "the origin of the office of the Governor came in existence when Queen Elizabeth (1558-1603) granted the trading powers to the Company of Merchants of London into the East Indies under the famous charter of 31st December 1660".[1] Under the charter Act of 1698 which defines the powers of the Governor provides "each president of the company was brought under the control of the Governor and Council appointed by the commission of the Company".[2]

"The Regulating Act of 1773 brought the Governors of Bombay and Madras under the control or supervision of the Governor General of Bengal. Even after this, Governors were masters in their respective presidencies and enjoyed plenty of powers. They also continued to enjoy the right of correspondence with the Board of Directors in the concerning matters about peace and war which made the position of the Governor General ineffective".[3]

"The Company's rule in India came to an end under the Government of India Act 1858. Consequently, the administration of India was transferred from the Company to the Crown in which India was to be governed by and in the name of Her Majesty".[4]

With the passing of the Provincial Autonomy under the Government of India Act 1935 "The whole executive authority of a Province was vested in the Governor".[5] Under this Act, "he was to act as a constitutional head of an autonomous Province and also to act as an agent of the Central Government especially when he was to act either in his discretion or in his individual judgment".[6] All the Legislative powers were also entrusted to him. In short the Governors were the real constitutional heads of the concerned provincial administration.

Discussion in the Constituent Assembly of India

The Constituent Assembly formed by the elected members in July 1946 for the formation of the Constitution of Indian discussed from the very beginning for the office of the Governor and all the members were unanimous on the view that the Governor should be the head of an Indian State.

The members of the Constituent Assembly adopted the document of the Constitution of India on November 26, 1949 and the Constitution of India came into force on the 26th January 1950. Article 153 of the Constitution of India provides that there shall be a Governor for each State. Again, Article 154(1) states, "The executive power of the state shall be vested in the Governor and shall be exercised either directly or through officers subordinate to him in accordance with this Constitution."

As head of the federating State, the Governor plays multi-faceted roles. The different roles can be discussed as follows:

1. The Governor as a Legislative Head.
2. The Governor as an Executive Head.
3. The Governor as a Judicial Head.
4. The Governor as a Financial Head.
5. The Governor and State Public Services.
6. The Governor as Chancellor of the University.

The Governor as a Legislative Head

The Governor is the head of the State Legislature. The Constitution of India provides the Governor of every State immense legislative power. For example,

(1) The Governor has the right to summon the State Legislature, prorogue either House and dissolve the Legislative Assembly as provided under Article 174.
(2) Article 175 states that the Governor may address either the House or both Houses of the Legislative Assembly. He may send messages to the House of the Legislature of the State with respect of a Bill pending in the State Legislature or any other matter.
(3) Article 200 provides that every Bill passed by the State Legislature has to receive the assent of the Governor before it can become a law.
(4) Under Article 201 he can reserve a bill for the consideration of the President.
5) Under Article 213, the Governor can promulgate ordinance during the recess of the Legislature. The Governor also nominates some members to the Legislative Council.

The Governor as an Executive Head

The Governor is the executive head of the State. The most important executive power of the Governor is the appointment of the State

Chief Minister and other ministers on the advice of the Chief Minister under Article 164 of the Constitution of India.

The Governor as a Judicial Head

The Governor also acts as the Judicial Head of the State. Under Article 161 of the Constitution of India, the Governor of a State shall have the power of grant to pardon, respite or remission of punishment or to suspend, remit or commutes the sentence of any person convicted of any offence against any law relating to a matter to which the executive power of the State extends. Thus the Governor is above the High Court of the State and acts as a judicial head.

The Governor as a Financial Head

The Governor is also the financial head of the State. All the financial matters of the State administration are performed after getting the approval of the Governor. Under Article 202 of the Constitution of India, the Governor has to lay the annual financial statement before the House or Houses of the Legislature. Under Article 203 also the Demand for Grant is made on the recommendation of the Governor. He can also cause to lay before the Legislature all the statements for Supplementary or Additional Expenditure or Demands for Excess Grants under Article 205. Article 207 states that all money bills can be introduced only on the recommendation of the Governor and any bill which requires expenditure from the consolidated fund of the State shall not be passed without the recommendation of the Governor.

The Governor and State Public Services

The Governor of the Indian States is the head of the State Public Services. Under Article 316(1) of the Constitution of India, the Governor appoints the Chairman and the other members of the State Public Service Commission. The appointments made by the Commission are in the name of the Governor. Other important public services of the State are also made in the name of the Governor. Administrative System in accordance to the needs of the changing society can be adopted by the Governor in consultation with the ministers and the heads of the departments. The improvement or the betterment of the public administration in the State also are to be examined by the Governor through the heads of the departments and the ministers. The Governor performs all his administrative functions through the legislative agency. The address given by the Governor for every year and just after every election contains the policy and programmes to be performed by the various departments in the coming years. The Address of the Governor is discussed in the Legislative Assembly under the title of "the debate on Governor's Address". From this debate the Governor can modify his target in running public administration to a great extent. Because in this debate, the MLAs mainly the opposition MLAs got chance to point out the loopholes and drawbacks of the functions of the Government. If the MLAs are correct and clear, the Governor can change and modify the public services for the satisfaction of the people through the ruling government.

The Governor as Chancellor of the University

The Governor as the head of the State performs the functions of the Chancellor of the University. His position in the University is not provided by the Constitution of India. There is also no uniform convention regarding his role in the University. But as a common practices, the Governor acts as the Chancellor of the University. This practice is not a new phenomena in India. "Even before Independence of India, the British Governors functioned as the Chancellors of the universities. For the first time, three universities were opened in India in the year 1857 under which the visitorial powers were vested in the governors as Chancellors of the Universities".[7] Every Chancellor of the University Act framed by the State Assembly. The power and functions of the Chancellor varies from University to University. But we can examine some common powers enjoyed by the Governor of the University.

(1) Legislative Power

The Governor as Chancellor of the University has to approve the proceedings of the executive body of the University. He has also to approve the appointment made in the University. The Chancellor is empowered to annul the wrong proceedings or appointments of the University which are not in accordance with the provision of the University Act or the statutes or the ordinances of the University. For example in 1971, the Chancellor of Agra University "cancelled the appointment of Dr. A.S. Mathur as the Director of the Institute of Social Sciences in the Agra University".[8]

The Chancellor has the power to approve drafts, statutes, ordinances, etc. passed by the Senate or any other bodies of the University. Sometimes the Vice-Chancellor reserved certain drafts, statutes and ordinances for the consideration of the Chancellor.

(2) Executive Power

(i) Under the written Constitution or Act of the University the Chancellor is empowered to appoint the Vice-Chancellor of the University or Universities in the State.

(ii) He also appoints the Finance Officer, Treasurer and other important officers in the University.

(iii) The Chancellor has the right to nominate dignified personality when the office of the Vice-Chancellor falls vacant in the University. He can appoint the Dean of any faculty or any other person as the Vice-Chancellor of the University.

(iv) He can interfere in the internal affairs of the University like (a) the fixation of the date for the convocation of the University, (b) offer of honorary degree, (c) opening of new departments, institutions, colleges, etc., and (d) he presides over the convocation of the University.

(3) Judicial Power

All the disputes within the institution are settled by the Chancellor whose decision is final.

(4) Financial Power

Funds, accounts, budget, etc., of the University are to be finalized after getting the approval of the Chancellor.

In exercising the powers and functions of the Chancellor there arises a question, i.e., is the Governor bound by the Ministerial advice? In this regard there are two different opinions. The opinion of one section is that the Governor is bound by the advice of the State Chief Minister in the affairs of the University. The group opines that the ministers who are the representatives of the people know better than the Governor, who usually comes from outside the State, the affairs of the University. On this ground a Chief Minister of Bombay once said, "a Chancellor cannot be a Chancellor unless he is the Governor and a Governor is bound to be guided by the advice of his ministers".[9]

MANIPUR

Manipur was under different rulers with different titles as head of the state. "Upto the reign of Charairongba (1698-1709) there were several independent kingdoms, namely, Moirang, Luwang, Mangang, Changlei, Khaba-Nganba, Ningthouja and Angom. Whenever they were threatened by any foreign aggression, they united together against the common enemy. Thus there was confederation".[10] The combination of the different kingdoms for their protection indicates very easily that they had a common head. Further L.W. Shakespeare in his book *History of Assam Rifles* mentions, "The Meitheis were the strongest of several clans inhabiting the Manipur Valley, who eventually obtained the mastery and gave their name to all other clans".[11] The strongest clan conquered the weaker one and annexed the territory through aggression. Later on the political system of Manipur was federal in character. Important powers and functions were concentrated in the hands of the Meitei king. The other six kingdoms were the federating units. The Meitei king assumed the role of the Emperor.[12] The heads of the six kingdoms were just like the Governors of the federating units of the present political system. There was also delegation of powers to the other heads of the units. "The emperor who was head of the seven kingdoms acted as the head of the federation. The head of other clans were autonomous in their respective areas".[13]

With the arrival of the British to Manipur in 1891, the power of the Maharaja of Manipur had reduced as they tried to capture political power in the State. From 1819 to 1826, the king of Manipur took help from the British to liberate Manipur from the Burmese invaders. Step by step the British began to control over Manipur and in 1891, the control was completed and made Manipur a part of the British Empire. Consequently, the Manipur Maharaja became only a titular head of the state. Even the coronation of Maharaja of Manipur was done by the British. "In 1891, Churachand Singh.... was appointed by the British as the king of Manipur".[14] "The king only enjoyed supremacy in the internal administration of the State and the conduct of external affairs, communication, defence and coinage were controlled by the British".[15] During the Kingship of Churachand Maharaja, the Council of Ministers, i.e., the Mantry system was replaced by a Durbar. The appointment and removal of members of the Durbar was in the hands of the Political Agent. Every resolution passed by the Durbar required the approval of the Maharaja. He could not return any resolution or bill for the reconsideration of the Durbar.[16] From this it is clear that the real administration was performed by the political Agent. This system of administration continued upto 15th August, 1947, the day of Indian Independence.

Under the Manipur State Constitution Act 1947, the administration of Manipur was vested in the Maharaja. All rights, authority and jurisdiction which appertain or are incidental to the Government are exercisable by the Maharaja subject to the provision of the Act. With the integration of Manipur into the Indian Union, Manipur became a Part 'C' State in the Constitution of India. An Advisory Council was instituted in the State. During the period of Advisory Council from 1951 to 1956, from 1st January 1957, the Advisory form of Government was substituted by the Territorial Council, consisting of 30 elected and two nominated members by the Seventh Amendment Act of the Constitution of India. Again, the Government of Union Territories Act 1963 was enacted by Parliament. The administration of Manipur was carried under the supervision of the Central Government. At that time, there was no head of State.

The Chief Commissioner took the charge of the administration of the State. Under the Government of Union Territories Act 1963, Manipur was headed by the Administrator having enormous powers and functions, viz., (1) Legislative power, (2) Executive power, (3) Financial power, and (4) Judicial power.

Legislative Power

As head of the State, the administrator of Manipur had the power to summon, prorogue and dissolve the Assembly".[17] He also has the power to address the Legislative Assembly and to send messages to the Assembly whether with respect to Bill then pending in the Assembly or otherwise, and when a message is so sent, the Assembly shall consider any matter required by the messages to be taken into consideration".[18] Further all the relevant functions of the Legislature of the State are done in the name of the administrator.

Executive Power

The Government of Union Territories Act 1963 provides immense executive power to the Administrator. The Act mentions "in case of difference of opinion between the Administrator and his ministers on any matter the Administrator shall refer it to the President for decision".[19] All the executive functions of the Union Territory are run by the administrator with the approval of the President of India.

Judicial Power

The Administrator of the Union Territory of Manipur discharged all the judicial functions of the Union Territory with the approval of the President.

Financial Power

Any financial bill shall not be introduced into or moved in the Legislative Assembly except on the recommendation of the Administrator.

The members of the Manipur Legislative Assembly and Council of Ministers though elected by the people of Manipur had no sufficient power in the administration of the State as the decision of the administrator was always final.

The State of Manipur was inaugurated by the Prime Minister Indira Gandhi on the 21st January 1972. As a full fledged State of the Indian Union. From that day, the head of the State of Manipur is the Governor, appointed by the President of India under his hand and seal for a period of five years.

Governor

The reason why the institution of the Governor seems to move from the confine of the Constitution to a subject of academic polemic is the role of the Governor himself as head of the State. The role of the Governor of Manipur is also becoming very significant in the administrative affairs of the State. Being the head of the State, his role may be discussed as follows:

(1) Governor as a Legislative Head,
(2) Governor as an Executive Head,
(3) Governor as a Judicial Head,
(4) Governor as a Financial Head,
(5) Governor and Manipur Public Services,
(6) Governor as Chancellor of the Manipur University, and
(7) Governor and Hill Areas.

The Governor as a Legislative Head

The Governor of Manipur enjoys immense legislative powers. But nomination of members in the Legislative Council which is one of the most important powers of the Governor is not exercised by him. Because the legislature of the State is a unicameral one and the practice of reservation of seats of the Anglo-Indian Community if they are not elected is not prevailing in Manipur. The Legislative powers of the Governor can be examined only on the following grounds:

(a) Summoning the Legislative Assembly,
(b) Address to the Assembly,
(c) Dissolution of the Assembly,
(d) Assent to Bills,
(e) To return the Bills,
(f) Preservation of Bills for the consideration of the President, and
(g) Promulgation of Ordinances.

(a) Summoning the Legislative Assembly

The Governor summons the Manipur Legislative Assembly from time to time.

(b) Address to the Assembly

In accordance with Article 176 of the Constitution of India, the Governor of Manipur as head of the Legislature gives his Address in every first session or sitting of the House of every year and in the first sitting of the House after every General Assembly Elections in the State. The address is prepared by the Council of Ministers and is composed of (i) the achievement of the Government; and (ii) the plans and programmes of the State administration to be adopted in the coming year. "K.V. Krishna Rao, the fourth Governor of Manipur in the sitting of the Fourth Manipur Legislative Assembly session of the Congress(I) Ministry under the Chief Ministership of Rishang Keishing on the 23rd February 1987 gave the introductory part of his Address in Meeteilon (Manipuri version) for the first time in the history of Manipur Legislative Assembly".[20] Similarly, on the 16th March 1988, in the first sitting of the Manipur Legislative Assembly during the time of the R.K.

Jaichandra led Congress(I) Government, the Governor himself again introduced his Address in Meeteilon (Manipur version)".[21]

(c) Dissolution of the Assembly

Under Article 174(2)(b) of the Constitution of India, the Governor has the right to dissolve the Legislative Assembly on the recommendation of the Chief Minister. Sometimes the Governor exercises his discretion to whether the Legislative Assembly is to be dissolved or not to be dissolved. For example, in 1973, when the United Legislative Party led by Alimuddin became minority due to defection "the Congress led Progressive Democratic Alliance met the Governor and requested him to allow them to form the ministry. But the Governor refused and on his recommendation the President dissolved the Assembly on 28th March 1973 and took over the administration of the State". Here the Governor might allow the Progressive Democratic Alliance to form the ministry but he really exercised his discretion because the President Rule was imposed in Manipur in spite of the 31 existing members of the Progressive Democratic Alliance in the Legislative Assembly.

(d) Assent to the Bills

Under Article 168 of the Constitution of India, the Governor of Manipur is an integral part of the State as the article stated that for every State there shall be a Legislature which consists of the Governor, and the Legislative Assembly of the State (and the Legislative Council if any). The Governor plays a significant role in making the laws of the State through the medium of his assent to the Bills under Article 200 of the Constitution of India. Under this Article the Governor of Manipur simply gives his assent to the bill for becoming a law. All the laws prevailing in the State had become so after taking the assent of the Governor. Sometimes, he withholds his assent to the bill which will affect the general interest after becoming law in the State.

(e) To Return the Bills

The Governor has the right to return the bills (except the money bills) for the reconsideration of the House with a message in the light of suggestion that the bill be reconsidered or modified. In 1984, Manipur Governor, Gen. K.V. Krishna Rao had returned a bill entitled the Manipur Rifle Police Force Bill by stating—"It appears to me the clause 5(2) has been put in a negative form and not happily worded."

Regarding the returning of bills, the returned bill is again passed by the House with or without the amendments proposed by the Governor, he has a right to withhold his assent.

(f) Preservation of Bills for the Consideration of the President

The Governor has also the right to preserve for the consideration of the President any bill with the Governor rationally thinks that after becoming law of the State would affect the existing law of the Union or violate the provisions of the Constitution or would disturb the law and order of the State or any part thereof. In 1978, the Manipur Language Official Bill which was passed by the Legislative Assembly on the 31st March 1978 was reserved by the then Governor L.P. Singh for the consideration of the President. In this connection the Governor might be thinking that the hill people of Manipur might launch any kind of strikes which may hinder the State administration.

(g) Promulgation of Ordinances

The Governor of Manipur becomes the sole legislative body in the State when the Legislative Assembly is not in session. He promulgates ordinances which can become the law of the State if the Legislative Assembly approves them when it is in session. Sometimes the ordinances were issued on the advice of the Council of Ministers. In Manipur Ordinances were promulgated from 1975 only. In 1975 the Governor L.P. Singh during the Chief Ministership of R.K. Dorendra Singh promulgated two ordinances, viz., the Manipur Legislature [(Removal of Disqualification) Amendment] Ordinance 1975 and the Manipur Land Reforms Ordinance 1975. In 1976, the Governor L.P. Singh promulgated five ordinances, namely, (a) the Departmentalization of Union Accounts (Transfer of Personnel, 1976; (b) The Manipur Co-operative Societies Ordinance 1976; (c) The Manipur Land Revenue and Land Reforms (Validation of Proceedings) Ordinance 1976; and (d) The Manipur Agricultural Credit Operation and Miscellaneous Provision (Banks) Ordinance 1976; and (e) The Metal Corporation (Nationalisation and Miscellaneous Provisions) Ordinance 1976. In 1977, two Ordinances (i) The Police (Manipur Third Amendment) Ordinance 1977; and (ii) the Disputed Elections (Prime Minister and Speaker) Ordinance 1977 were promulgated by the Governor L.P. Singh during the Janata Rule in the State and under the Chief Ministership of Yang Maso Shaiza. The same Governor in 1978 promulgated another 3 Ordinances namely (i) The Manipur Municipalities (Second Amendment) Ordinance, 1978, (ii) The Manipur Public Premises (eviction of unauthorized occupants) ordinance 1978; and (iii) The Manipur Parliamentary Secretary (Salary and Allowance) Ordinances 1978; and in 1979 another three Ordinances, viz., (i) The Manipur Highway Ordinance 1979, (ii) The Representation of the People (Amendment) Ordinance 1979, and (iii) The Manipur Panchayat Raj (Second Amendment) Ordinance 1979.

In 1980, during the Congress(I) led coalition ministry led by R.K. Dorendra, the Governor L.P. Singh Promulgated three Ordinance namely, (i) The Manipur Preventive Detention Ordinance 1980, (ii) The Manipur State Housing Board Ordinance 1980, and (iii) The Salary and Allowances of Chairman of the Manipur Legislative Assembly (Hill Areas Committee) (Amendment) Ordinance 1980. The Governor S.M. Burney promulgated one Ordinance in 1981—the Manipur Municipalities (Fourth Amendment) Ordinance 1981, two in 1982 namely, (i) The Manipur University (Amendment) Ordinance 1982, and (ii) The Disturbed Areas (Special Court) (Manipur Amendment) Ordinance 1982. In

1983, the Governor also promulgated four Ordinances (i) The Manipur Secondary Education (Third Amendment) Ordinance 1983, (ii) The Manipur Professions, Trades, Callings and Employment Taxation (Second Amendment) Ordinance 1983, (iii) The Salary and Allowances of Members of the Legislative Assembly (Manipur) (Eighth Amendment) Ordinance 1983, and (iv) The Manipur Panchayati Raj (Third Amendment) Ordinance 1983".

Governor as Executive Head

The role of the Governor as Executive head of the State can be discussed under two grounds—(i) Appointment of the Chief Minister, and (ii) Resignation and removal of the Chief Minister.

(i) Appointment of the Chief Minister

After every General Assembly elections of the State the Chief Minister is appointed by the Governor, the leader of the party getting majority in the election. When only one political party secures majority in the newly elected Assembly of the State or a coalition of parties getting a clear leader, the role of the Governor in appointing the Chief Minister becomes very important. When no political party is able to command majority in the State Legislature, the Governor has to follow two types of practices in the appointment of the Chief Minister. The practices are:

(i) To assess the different claimants from the different political parties: After assessing the claims and counter claims the Governor has to invite the leader who, according to different parties could command a majority in the Assembly.

(ii) To invite the leader of the largest single party in the Assembly to form the Government without assessing the claims and counterclaims.

In a coalition of different political parties the assessment of the leader who is to be appointed as Chief Minister is very significant. There are two modes of assessment as (a) List system, and (b) Physical Verification system. In the list system, the Governor has to see the list submitted by the party leader containing the respective supports. He will verify the loyalty of the party members in the list. Here he will appoint the leader of the party having largest number of members as Chief Minister.

In the physical verification system, the Governor cannot satisfy only in the list of the party members submitted by the respective leaders. In Manipur, on 20 March, 1972, just after the statehood of the State on 21 January 1972, the United Legislature Party led by the Manipur Peoples Party formed the Government after the Governor B.K. Nehru had physically verified the members. The ULP "Minister is headed by Md. Alimuddin and consisted of 15 MPP, 3 SSP, 1 Congress(O) and 13 Independents". Again in 1974, when there was a rift in the then Progressive Democratic Ministry comprising Congress(I), CPI, MHU and Manipur Democratic Party (those MLAs defected from ULP), L.P. Singh, the Governor of Manipur did not allow them to form the government by showing the list of the MLAs. A group of Congress members negotiated with the ULP and "could collect only 31 members on the side. They have personally shown themselves to the Governor, on the other hand, would not allow them to form the Ministry by the 31 members". The Congress thereupon claimed that "three members of the Congress party were kept under duress in the camp of Yangmaso Shaiza and requested the Governor to see them personally and take their opinion. The Governor called the three members to Raj Bhavan and took their statements in which they had expressed their support to the Congress-ULP coalition". From the physical verification, the Governor advised Shaiza to resign. Consequently, the Shaiza ministry resigned on 5th December 1974. Thus under the physical verification system L.P. Singh appointed R.K. Dorendro Singh as Chief Minister of the Democratic Legislative Party on the 6th December 1974. Moreover, the Governor as head of the State may also ask the Chief Minister to face the Assembly within a specified period.

After the Lok Sabha Election of March 1977, there was large scale defection in Manipur. Consequently, the ruling Congress Party was reduced to a minority. In the month of June the strength of Janata Party had increased to more than 50 in a House of 60 members. "On 29th June, Yang Maso Shaiza, the Janata MP (defecting from Congress) was sworn in as the first Chief Minister of Janata Government in Manipur by the then Governor L.P. Singh".[28]

In the Assembly elections of January 1980, no party secured majority in the Legislative Assembly of Manipur. But the Congress(I) Party was able to collect MLAs from the Congress (U), MPP, KNA and Independents in order to form a coalition ministry. The Governor L.P. Singh could easily invite as Chief Minister the leader of the Congress(I) Party, R.K. Dorendro Singh to form a coalition ministry.

"In 1988, on 5th March at 30 minutes after mid-night, R.K. Jaichandra, the former Union Minister of Chemical and Petro-Chemical (State) was sworn as the Chief Minister of Manipur at Raj Bhavan by the Governor K.V. Krishna Rao"[29] by dismissing the then Chief Minister Rishang Keishing. Thus, the Governor being an executive head of the State can appoint a Chief Minister even at night.

In 1990, February Assembly Elections, no party secured majority. But Congress(I) became the largest single party securing 26 members. On the other hand, the United Front was formed by opposition parties, viz., Janata Dal, MPP, Congress(S), CPI, KNA, CPI(M) and NPP. The Front claimed that "it had the support of 32 MLAs".[30] R.K. Dorendro Singh the leader of the Congress(I) party also requested the Governor, Chintamani Panigrahi under the influence of the Central political leaders P. Upendra, George Fernandes, etc., invited R.K. Ranbir Singh, the leader of the United Front to form the Government.[31]

(ii) Resignation and Removal of the Chief Minister/Ministers

The resignation of the Chief Ministers are to be made through the Governor of the State. The Governor should dismiss whole ministry if it does not resign even after a clear vote of no confidence has been passed against it. In other words, if the Government ceases to have a majority, the Chief Minister has to resign immediately. If he does not do so, the Governor should dismiss him. In Manipur the MPP led U.L.P. coalition government under the leadership of Md. Alimuddin lost majority support on March 1973. The Progressive Democratic Alliance formed by the Congress, CPI and PIG could collect 32 MLAs and "a no-confidence motion was moved on 26 March, 1973. The Chief Minister submitted his resignation of his ministry to the Governor"[32] before the Governor had dismissed the ministry. In 1974 also the opposition took quite a different strategy to overthrow the MPP led the United Legislature Party and "when the Manipur Appropriation (No. 3) Bill 1974 was taken up for clause by clause consideration and after voting it was defeated by 3 to 1 votes. In the meantime, Md. Alimuddin met the Governor and handed over the resignation of his Council of Ministers in the afternoon of the 8th July 1974".[33] Again the Democratic Legislature Party (Congress and ULP) Chief Minister "R.K. Dorendro requested the Governor to allow him to form a pure Congress Ministry. After getting favourable response from the Governor, R.K. Dorendro tendered the resignation of his DLP Ministry on 23 July 1974"[34] and was sworn in as Chief Minister of the Congress-CPI coalition ministry on the same day. Here the Governor used his discretion in making resignation of the Chief Minister for the formation of another ministry.

The Janata Government of Manipur formed on the 29th June 1977 under the Chief Ministership of Yang Maso Shaiza was dismissed for the first time in Manipur on November 1979 by the Governor L.P. Singh. The dismissal was caused by many factors like:

(i) Defection of 9 MLAs led by R.K. Dorendro Singh from the party,

(ii) Demand of the CPI for immediate resignation of the Janata Ministry on the ground of declaration of the whole of Manipur valley as a disturbed area and the use of the most hated Armed Forces (Assam and Manipur) Special Power Act 1958.

(iii) Launching of *Satyagraha* movement by the Congress Party from September 1978.

(iv) "Eight political parties of Manipur, i.e., the Congress, the Congress(I), the CPI, the CPI(M), the Lok Dal, the Manipur Peoples' Party, the Ereibak Leishem Party and the Kuki National Assembly unanimously resolved to urge the President, N. Sanjiva Reddy and the Central leaders to dissolve the out lived Manipur Legislative Assembly and dismissal of the Janata Ministry".[35]

The Congress(I) led coalition Ministry under the Chief Ministership of R.K. Dorendro Singh of 1980 also faced a political crisis caused mainly by defection of 11 members to the opposition. Consequently the Governor L.P. Singh dismissed the Chief Minister and his ministry. The Congress Ministry of 1984 led by Rishang Keishing created a dissident politics within the party itself on the ground of money allegations like the corruption activities of the Chief Minister. Inspite of many charges of corruption Rishang Keishing enjoyed absolute majority in the Assembly. But only on March 1988, the Governor K.V. Krishna Rao under the Central direction dismissed the Rishang Keishing Ministry on the ground that he had supported insurgency in Manipur.

The Governor as a Judicial Head

The Governor of Manipur is the judicial head of the State. In the Rule of Business, there are some judicial head of the State. In the Rule of Business, there are some judicial cases to be submitted to the Governor of Manipur. They are:

(a) "proposals for the grant of pardons of commutation of sentence in pursuance of Article 161".[36]

(b) "Cases relating to petitions for mercy from or on behalf of person sentenced to death".[37]

(c) "Proposals for awarding major punishments of dismissal or removal or compulsory retirement from service".[38]

(d) "Proposals for awarding major punishments to the Gazetted officers under Manipur Services (Discipline and Appeal) Rules in force".[39]

From these rules it is clear that the Governor of Manipur possess immense judicial power as head of the State.

The Governor as a Financial Head

The Governor of Manipur is also the financial head of the State. The Annual Financial Statement of the State is to be laid before the Legislative Assembly by the Governor under Article 202 of the Constitution of India. The Governor of Manipur also has to recommend the Demand for Grant under Article 203 of the Constitution. Under Article 205, he can lay the statements for Supplementary or Additional Expenditure or Demands of Excess Grant of the State. All the money bills of the State can be introduced only on the recommendation of the Governor of Manipur as provided in Article 207 of the Constitution of India. Again, any bill which requires expenditure from the Consolidated Fund of the State of Manipur shall not be passed without the recommendation of the Governor. In other words, all the financial matters of the State are to be run on the approval of the Governor as he is the real financial head of the State.

The Governor as Chancellor of the Manipur University

Like other Governors of the Indian States, the Governor of Manipur is the Chancellor of the Manipur University. He enjoys immense powers and functions in running the administration of the University as provided by the Manipur University Act. In the hierarchical administrative structure of the Manipur University, the Chancellor is at the apex while the Senate and syndicate which are legislative body and the executive body respectively are at the lower level. "The Chancellor shall be the head of the University and the President of the Senate".[40]

As head of the University, the powers and functions of the Chancellor can be discussed under the following heads:

(1) Legislative Power.
(2) Executive Power.
(3) Judicial Power, and
(4) Financial Power.

The Legislative Power

The Manipur University Act empowers the Chancellor of the Manipur University to make laws and regulations of the University:

(1) "Every new statute or addition to the statute shall require the approval of the Chancellor who may assent thereto or withhold assent or remit to the syndicate for reconsideration".[41]
(2) "a new statute or a statute amending or repealing an existing statute shall have no validity unless it has been assented to by the Chancellor".[42]
(3) In regard to the making of Ordinances of the University, the Chancellor of the Manipur University has immense power. The Act mentions "All ordinances made by the Syndicate shall be submitted as soon as may be, to the Chancellor and the Senate".[43]
(4) Again, "the Chancellor may by order, direct that the operation of any Ordinance shall be suspended until he has had an opportunity of exercising his power of disallowance and any order of suspension under this clause shall cease to have effect on the expiration of one month from the date of such order or on the expiration of fifteen days from the date of consideration of the Ordinance by the Senate, whichever period expires later".[44]
(5) In another clause, it is further mentioned, "the Chancellor, within three months after any Ordinance has been

considered by the Senate, signify to the Syndicate his disallowance of the Ordinance, and from the date of receipt by the Syndicate of intimation of such disallowance, the Ordinance shall cease to have effect".[45] Moreover, "the Chancellor may by order in writing annul any proceeding of the University which is not in conformity with this act, the statutes or the Ordinances. Provided that before making any such order, the Chancellor shall call upon the University to show cause any such order should not be made, and shall consider the cause if any is shown within a reasonable time".[46]

The Executive Power

The Chancellor of the Manipur University is the real Executive head of the institution. All the executive functions of the University are discharged with the approval of the Chancellor. The Manipur University Act confers innumerable executive powers to the Chancellor. The Executive power of the Chancellor can be analysed as follows:

(1) The Chancellor is the President of the Senate under Section 9, Clause 1 of the Manipur University Act 1980. Consequently, he presides the meetings of the Senate by giving address. Here we can mention some address given by the Chancellor in the meetings of the Senate of the University:

(a) "Recent years have witnessed significant changes in our system, approaches and also the expansion of policies connected with education... However, this relatively bright picture is simultaneously afflicted by visible inability to satisfy certain visible inality to satisfy certain requisites and some daunting challenges. It is in the sphere that this Senate, as the Policy Formulator, Friend, Philosopher and Guide of the Academic Community and the students of the State, in a position to consider possible alternatives and to provide solutions to what I have preferred to refer as 'Requisites and Challenges".[47]

(b) "I have occasion to emphasize that our duty should primarily revolve round the imperative state in Education a strong point for the society.... I very strongly feel that to achieve the 'Goals' we are seeking, the results of education must always be subjected to consciously stiff scrutiny continuously so that future generations may get the benefit of the 'Collective Wisdom' of August forums like Senate".[48]

(2) "The Registrar of the University supplies to the Chancellor copies of the agenda of meeting of the authorities of the University as soon as they are assured and the minutes of the meeting of the authorities ordinarily within a month of the holding of the meeting".[49]

(3) "The Chancellor may from time to time, appoint one or more persons to review the work and progress of the University and to submit a report thereon, and upon receipt of the report, the chancellor, may after obtaining the views of the Syndicate thereon, take such action and issue such directions as he considers necessary in respect of any of the matters dealt with in the report and the University shall be bound to comply with such direction".[50]

(4) "The Chancellor shall also have the right to cause an inspection to be such person or persons, as he may direct, of the University, its building, as he may direct, of the University and also of the examinations, teaching and other work conducted or done by the University and to cause an inquiry to be made in respect of any matter in connection with the University".[51] In relation to examination system, under this power, the Chancellor of the Manipur University mentioned in one of his address as, "In my capacity as the Governor of the State, I have received disturbing report about malpractices and indiscipline occurring during the recently concluded pre-University examinations. An

obvious remedy would be to make it compulsory for the students to sit as examinees in any institution but their own. A regular system of sending the answer scripts of all University examinations like pre-University, examinations like pre-University, B.A. and B.Sc. and M.Sc. This will, no doubt help raise the standards and will also ensure fair assessment of performances".[52]

(5) "The Chancellor shall in every case give notice to the University of his intention to cause an inspection of inquiry".[53]

(6) After the inspection is over, "the Chancellor may address the Vice-Chancellor with reference to the result of such inspection and inquiry, and the Vice-Chancellor shall communicate to the syndicate. The views of the chancellor with such advice as the Chancellor may offer upon the action to be taken thereon".[54]

(7) "The Vice-Chancellor shall be appointed by the Chancellor from a panel of not less than three persons who shall be recommended by a committee consisting of three members.

Provided that if the Chancellor does not approve of any of the person so recommended".[55]

(8) "The Chancellor, shall if present, preside at the convocation of University for conferring degrees and all meetings of the Senate".[56] In this connection some of the addresses delivered by the Chancellor in the convocations may be mentioned: (a) "To begin with, the University and the teaching community, functioning as Counsellors and Motivators, should be able to effectively initiate the wanted process of psychology reorientation of the attitude of the education unemployed".[57] (b) "My advice to the students would be that they must make full use of the available facilities and of those being introduced by the University. I would also like to emphasize that the education that they are getting is meant for the benefit of the country and, therefore, they must consciously evolve attitude which would make them outgiving, competitive and forward

looking. The whole country is their job market and they must utilize the innumerable opportunity being thrown up by our developmental effort".[58]

(9) "If the Syndicate and Academic Council shall be nominated by the Chancellor and may hold office for a term of three years".[59]

(10) "If the Syndicate purpose to make an appointment otherwise than in the order of merit arranged by the Selection Committee in the post of Professor, Reader or Lecturer,[60] it shall record its reasons in writing and submit them to the Chancellor who may approve to proposal or return it to the Syndicate for reconsideration. After reconsideration, if the Syndicate desires to pursue its original proposal, it shall refer the matter again to the Chancellor for his decision which shall be final".[61]

(11) Except the Vice-Chancellor, "other members of the Planning Board shall be appointed by the Chancellor and shall hold office for such period as he may determine".[62]

(12) The Chancellor, as head of the University presides other important, meetings and symposium. He also arranges for awarding medals, degrees, etc., in the University if he desires. We can cite some examples:

(a) "It may be recalled that as desired by His Excellency, the Governor of Manipur, Gen. K.V. Krishna Rao, the Annual Essay Competition for Governor's medal was introduced for the first time in 1984. The theme of the competition is for national integration and allied subjects. The competition has two categories: (i) Post Graduate students of Manipur University, and (ii) Under Graduate students of Manipur University. For each category three prizes of Gold, Silver and Bronze have to be awarded by His Excellency the Governor of Manipur for every year".[63]

(b) "The unlimited potential of the vast stretches of Hills have not yet received adequate attention. It would not be incorrect to surmise that, if the basis of balanced

> development were kept in view, the economy of the State would obviously entail effective participation of every area, whether in the Hills or in the Valley, in development process of the State".[64]

Judicial Power

The Chancellor as the head of the University settles disputed arises in the Constitution of the University authorities and bodies. The University Act also mentions "If any question arises whether any person has been duly elected or appointed as, or is entitled to be, a member of any authority or other body of the University, the matter shall be referred to the Chancellor whose decision thereon shall be final".[65]

Financial Power

The Chancellor of the Manipur University also enjoys financial power. The Act mentions—

(1) "The accounts, when audited shall be published by the syndicate in the Manipur Gazette, and a copy of the accounts together with the audit report shall be submitted by the Registrar to the Chancellor and to the Senate".[66]

(2) "The audited accounts and the annual financial estimates of the University shall be considered by the Senate in its annual meeting, and the Senate may pass resolutions thereon and communicate them to the Syndicate".[67] The Chancellor being the President of the Senate has full financial power under this Section too.

(3) "The Chancellor also nominated one person to the Finance Committee".[68]

Regarding his financial power, the Chancellor once said, "I have mentioned about the requirements of bounds for the University in the coming years. I have no doubt that the Government of India as well as the Government of Manipur would ensure that adequate funds are available during the Seventh Plan period. I, on my part, as your Chancellor or as the Governor of the State, shall spare no effort to contribute my mite in helping the University to prosper and develop".[69]

The Governor and the Manipur State Public Services

The Governor of Manipur is the head of all the State Public Services of Manipur. All the administrative heads and the other subordinates have close relationships with the Governor. The relationship may be termed as the employer-employee relationship. Because not only the Ministers of the State but also the State employees hold office during the pleasures of the Governor. All the appointments of the State administration of Manipur and transfers and resignation of the civil servant are made in the name of the Governor of the State.

The Manipur Public Service Commission was inaugurated by the first Manipur Governor B.K. Nehru on the 23rd October 1972. The Governor wanted the Commission to be a free and independent body so that there should be efficient administration in the State. So, the Governor in his inaugural speech of the State Public Service Commission said that "the Commission should work without any afraid of political pressure and sympathy. He further said that if the Ministers tried to influence the members of the Commission under political pressure they (members of the Commission) should say boldly that the process should not be used at all".[70]

Shri Nehru also said that "the task of the Service Commission is very important and responsive. Its function is to appoint efficient and qualified people. The Commission should appoint meritorious and men of integrity. The Commission should not be afraid of any political pressure because the ministers are temporary while the officers are permanent. The task of the Ministers is just like the work of a vehicle, policy will bring the vehicle at the desired way. It is the officers who will keep the vehicle to work efficiently".[71]

The services of the officers are governed by the elaborate Civil Service Rules made in the name of the Governor of Manipur. In the absence of the Ministry, i.e., during the President Rule, the

Governor has to supervise all the governments. Regarding the functioning of the employees, the Governor L.P. Singh in 1978 said:

(i) "The Manipur Government, Commissioner, Secretary and the head of departments have to keep justice and national integrity.

(ii) The officials have to visit the office in time and to look after their lower officials regularly.

(iii) If some one is discharging his official duty partially and use his official power wrongly, severe punishment should be imposed.

(iv) The wrongly made plans for the sake of the minority groups before the President's Rule should be brought out for taking scrutiny.

(v) The employees should use the sanctioned money for the development of the people within the allotted period and if used on reasonable ground, the State will get more money from the North Eastern Council and the Centre".[72]

The Governor of Manipur also tried to maintain active service in the State administration even in his absence. In 1980, L.P. Singh before his departure from Imphal had entrusted "the Border Security Force Director General, Sharwal Tandon, Assam rifles Director General, Lieutenant General Sushil Kumar and the General Officer Commanding Major General Venkata Rao to take up actions for the maintenance of peace in the State. He also met the State Chief Minister and other high officials of the State and said that instead of using larger number of security forces to control the problem in the State it is better to advice through conversation of mutual understanding with the young people".[73]

The Governor of Manipur being the administrative head in the State tried to improve the administrative system by consulting the different departments. It may be mentioned that "on the 10th May 1982, S.M. Burney, the Governor of Manipur chaired a high standard meeting at the Old Secretariat Conference Hall regarding the reformation of Administrative system in the State. Chief Minister Rishang Keishing, his Cabinet Ministers, Chief Secretary, I.G.P. Head of Departments, Deputy Commissioners, S.Ps., M.R. (Manipur Rifles) Commandants and top officials of army were present in the meeting. In the meeting different reports from all heads of departments were discussed".[74]

Sometimes the Governor has also taken action for the improvement of the law and order situation in the State. A local paper comments: "In the Secretariat Conference Hall, Imphal in 1984, a conference on law and order and development plan of administration was discussed for two days. The Governor K.V. Krishna Rao said that maintenance of peace, law and order, efficient administration will bring development in all respects only when the officers and employees work together then there will be a welfare State".[75]

The Governor of Manipur and the Tribal People

As head of the State the Governor of Manipur has a special responsibility for the tribal people of the State. The special attention of the head of State towards the hill people of Manipur had started from the time of Administrator in Manipur. It is proved by the existence of the Manipur Tribal Development Corporation Limited which was constituted under the Companies Act 1956 and the Tribal Welfare Department was established in 1968 by the Governor of Manipur in order to look after the backward sections of people of Manipur known as the Scheduled Tribes and Scheduled Castes. Large sums of money has been sanctioned for every year by the Government of Manipur for the betterment of this section of people. My schemes and plans were made under the Finance Commission for the development of the Scheduled Castes and Scheduled Tribes people of Manipur.

Gen. K.V. Krishna Rao, the Governor of Manipur in his inaugural address on a symposium in Manipur University said, "The unlimited potential of the vast stretches of hills have not yet received adequate attention. It would not be incorrect to surmise that if the basics of balanced development were kept in view, the economy of the State would obviously entail effective participation of every area, whether in the hills or in the valley, in the development process of the State".[76]

The Governor of Manipur sanctioned large amount of money for the tribal people of Manipur. For example, the Governor of Manipur has sanctioned a sum of rupees 1.50 lakhs for giving even special coaching (in science and mathematics) for the year 1983 in the hill areas of Manipur. "The object of this programme is that, it is seen generally that the tribal students are really weak in science and mathematics subjects. It is, therefore, found essential to give encouragement to these students who are at the High School stage by way of opening Special Coaching Centres for them in different places of the hill areas of the State".[77] Again, in order to raise the standard of the general education of the tribal people "the scheme of the general education had been taken in the State with a total outlay of ₹ 42.00 lakhs for the year, 1983-84.[78] The Governor really took great interest for the development of education programme for the Scheduled Caste and Scheduled Tribes. "during the year, 1984-85, a sum of ₹ 39.75 lakhs had been utilized against the total outlay of ₹ 40.00 lakhs for Scheduled Tribes and an amount of ₹ 165 lakhs for Scheduled Caste for the year 1984-85".[79]

For the establishment of village and small industries for the tribal people of Manipur "there is a provision of ₹ 20.00 lakhs for the year 1984-85. An amount of ₹ 20.00 lakhs was utilized during the year under report".[80] During the year 1985-86 also, an amount of ₹ 80.00 lakhs was made available under the State plan sector. With the availability of this amount, the Department registered the following achievements—

(i) Construction of 20 number of School Buildings in the Schoolless villages.
(ii) Award of Pre-Matric stipend to 186 Scheduled Tribes and Scheduled Caste students.
(iii) Construction of 5 number of Hostel buildings.
(iv) Construction of 11 number School buildings.

(v) Publication of 66 number of books in different tribal dialects.

(vi) Financial assistance to 238 schools for procurement of equipments.

(vii) Construction of 2 number of Community Halls at ₹ 3.50 lakhs each and 3 number of 6 Community Hall at ₹ 0.50 lakhs".[81]

"The Governor of Manipur in the year 1986-87 has also sanctioned an amount of ₹ 84.00 lakhs under the State Plan Sector for the implementation of various development programmes"[82] of the Tribal people. Similarly, "during the year under report an amount of ₹ 100.00 lakhs was made available under the State Plan Sector for implementation of various family Oriented Schemes and infrastructure schemes in the tribal areas of the State".[83]

The Governor of Manipur sometimes made monthly sanction on minimum amount for the tribal people according to time and situation. Some examples are given below:

(1) "The Governor of Manipur is pleased to accord administrative approval and expenditure sanction to an amount not exceeding ₹ 3,63,000 (₹ three lakhs and sixty three thousand) only for construction of Type II Quarters under the Eighth Finance Commission"[84] in the tribal areas of the State.

(2) "The Governor of Manipur is pleased to accord administrative approval and expenditure sanction to an amount not exceeding to ₹ 1,00,000 (₹ one lakhs) only for construction of Basket Ball Court at (1) Senapati, (2) Girls Hostel at Lemka College, Churachandpur, (3) Tamenglong Higher Seconary School Tamenglong, (4) Pettigrw College, Ukhrul, (5) the compound of Multipurpose Community Hall at Chandel"[85] for the tribal people.

(3) "The Governor of Manipur is pleased to accord administrative approval and expenditure sanction to an amount not exceeding to ₹ 1,00,000/- (₹ one lakh) only

for the construction of godown at Senapati District Head Quarters for the year 1988-89".[86]

(4) "The Governor of Manipur is pleased to accord administrative approval and expenditure sanction to an amount not exceeding to ₹ 17.00 lakhs (₹ Seventeen lakhs) only being the cost for construction of 3 (three) number of Scheduled Tribe Boy's Hostels at Churachandpur, Paomata and Ukhrul for the year 1988-89".[87]

(5) "The Governor of Manipur is pleased to accord administrative approval and expenditure sanction to an amount not exceeding to ₹ 3,15,000 (₹ three lakhs fifteen thousand) only for the establishment of the following 5 (five) Production-cum-Training for Knitting, Tailoring and Embroidery under Women and Children Programme for the year 1988-89 in the 5 Hill Districts—

Sl. No.	*Name & Address of the beneficiary Society*	*Name of District*	*Amount sanctioned*
1	*2*	*3*	*4*
1.	Hamajung Memorial Kniting and Tailoring works	Tamenglong	₹ 63,000
2.	Sangi Nool Knitting Centre	Churachandpur	₹ 63,000
3.	Tangkhul Shanao Long	Ukhrul	₹ 63,000
4.	Mao Naga Women Welfare Association, Tadubi	Senapati	₹ 63,000
5.	Aimol Chingnunghut	Chandel	₹ 63,000
	(₹ three lakhs fifteen thousand) only".[88]		₹ 3,15,000

(6) "The Governor of Manipur is pleased to accord administrative approval and expenditure sanction an amount not exceeding to ₹ 3,15,000 (₹ three lakhs fifteen thousand only) for the establishment of the following 5 (five) Production-cum-Training Centre for Type Writing one each in the 5 Hill Districts at ₹ 63,000 (₹ sixty three thousand) only per unit under Women and Children Programme for the year 1988-89.

Sl. No.	Name & Address of the beneficiary Society	Name of District	Amount sanctioned
1	2	3	4
1.	Pari Type Writing Centre Vungnuam Village	Churachandpur	₹ 63,000
2.	Society for Social and Moral Rearmament	Ukhrul	₹ 63,000
3.	Regional Training Development Institute	Chandel	₹ 63,000
4.	Vocational Speed Writer's School	Tamenglong	₹ 63,000
5.	Oklong Women Society	Senapati	₹ 63,000
	(₹ Three lakhs fifteen thousand) only"[89]		**₹ 3,15,000**

From the above facts and figures it is known that the Governor of Manipur, as head of the State has taken great care and attention for the development of the Scheduled Caste and Scheduled Tribe people of the State in all aspects of life irrespective of distance and sex.

References

1. Saharay H.K., '*Legal Study of Constitutional Development of India*', Nabha Ral Publishers, Calcutta, 1970, pp. 35-36.
2. *Ibid.*, pp. 37-38.
3. Sharma, Sri Ram, '*A Constitutional History of India*', Macmillan, Madras, 1954, 2nd Edn., pp. 28-29.
4. Banerjee, A.C. (Edt)., '*Indian Constitutional Documents*', Vol. II, A Mukherjee & Private Co., Calcutta, 1948, p. 3.
5. *Ibid.*, p. 279.
6. *Ibid.*, p. 296.
7. Dongerkery, S.R., *University Autonomy in India*, Lelvani Publishing House, Bombay, 1967, p. 32.
8. *The Statesman* (Delhi), 22.7.1971.
9. Dole, N.V., 'The Position of the Chancellor Governor in India', *The Journal of Political Science,* Vol. XXII, No. 184, Delhi University, January-December 1961, p. 379.
10. Ksh. Bimola, '*Government and Politics in Manipur 1950-80*', An unpublished Thesis submitted for the Degree of Ph.D. Gauhati University, Chapter II, p. 27.
11. Shakespeare, L.W., '*History of Assam Rifles,* MacMillian & Co. Ltd., St. Marines Street, London, 1929 Edn., p. 15.
12. Ksh. Bimola Devi, *op. cit.*, p. 27.

13. *Ibid.*, p. 29.
14. *Ibid.*, p. 31.
15. *Ibid.*, pp. 31-32.
16. *Ibid.*, p. 32.
17. *The Government of Union Territories Act 1963*, Section 6(1) (2).
18. *Ibid.*, Section 9(1)(2).
19. *Ibid.*, Section 44(1).
20. *Ibid.*, 2.4. 1987.
21. *Ibid.*, 17.3.1988.
22. *Simanta Patrika*, 29.3.1973.
23. *The Assembly Proceedings*, Vol. 4, Legislative Assembly Secretariat Manipur, February 25, 1985, p. 20.
24. The Government of Manipur, Law Department, *Ordinance*, 1984.
25. Th. Gokul Singh, '*Defection in Manipur*', Imphal, 1978, 1st Edition, pp. 40-41.
26. *Simanta Patrika*, 2.12.1974.
27. Th. Gokul Singh, *op. cit.*, p. 58.
28. *Amrita Bazar Patrika*, 30.5.77.
29. *Matam*, 8.3.88.
30. *Prajatantra*, 22.2.90.
31. *Huyen Lanpao*, 24.2.90.
32. Ksh. Bimola Devi. *op. cit.*, p. 164.
33. Th. Gokul Singh, *op. cit.*, p. 55.
34. Ksh. Bimola Devi, *op. cit.*, p. 171.
35. *Amrita Bazar Patrika*, 5.11.1979.
36. *Rules of Business of the Government of Manipur, Confidential and Cabinet Department, Government of Manipur Order*, Imphal, the 21st January, 1972.
37. *Ibid.*
38. *Ibid.*
39. *Ibid.*
40. *Manipur University Act 1980*, Section 9, Clause 1.
41. *Ibid.*, Section 18, Clause 3.
42. *Ibid.*, Clause 4.
43. *Ibid.*, Section 36, Clause 5.
44. *Ibid.*, Clause 6.
45. *Ibid.*, Clause 7.
46. *Ibid.*, Section 8, Clause 8.
47. Address by the Governor of Manipur Gen. K.V. Krishna Rao (Retd.) at the 9th meeting of the Senate of the Manipur University on May 22, 1988.

48. Address by Gen. K.V. Krishna Rao, Governor of Manipur at the 10th meeting of the Senate on 22 May 1989, Manipur University.
49. Manipur University Act, *op. cit.*, second schedule, section 7.
50. *Ibid.*, section 8, Clause 3.
51. *Ibid.*, section 8, Clause 3.
52. Address by the Governor of Manipur Gen. K.V. Krishna Rao (Retd.) at the second Senate Meeting on February 15, 1985, Manipur University.
53. Manipur University Act, *op. cit.*, section 8, Clause 4.
54. *Ibid..*, Clause 5.
55. *Ibid.*, section II, Clause I.
56. *Ibid.*, section 9, Clause 2.
57. Manipur University Bulletin May-June 1985, "Address by the Chancellor, K.V. Krishna Rao on the convocation on May 11, 1985.
58. *Ibid.*
59. Manipur University Act, *op. cit.*, Section 28(a).
60. *Ibid.*, Section 28(b)
61. *Ibid.*, Section 26, Clause 4.
62. *Ibid.*, Section 16, Clause 1.
63. Manipur University Bulletin, March/April, 1985, p. 18.
64. Inaugural Address by Gen. K.V. Krishna Rao (Retd.), Governor of Manipur on 'The Symposium on Manipur 2000 A.D. At Manipur University, 28th September 1985.
65. Manipur University Act, *op. cit.*, Section 23.
66. *Ibid.*, Section 22, Clause 2.
67. *Ibid.*, Section 22, Clause 3.
68. *Ibid.*, Second Schedule, Section 18, Clause I, III.
69. *Address by the Governor of Manipur Gen. K.V. KIrishna Rao (Retd.) in the Second Senate Meeting* of February 15, 1985, Manipur University.
70. *Simanta Patrika,* 24.10.1972.
71. *Prajatantra,* 24.10.1972.
72. *Simanta Patrika,* 20.11.1978.
73. *Prajatantra,* 12.5.1980.
74. *Khollao,* 11.5.1982.
75. Prajatantra, 5.9.1984.
76. *Inaugural Address by Gen. K.V. Krishna Rao (Retd.) on the Symposium on Manipur: 2000 A.D.* at the Manipur University dated September 28, 1985.
77. '*Annual Administrative Report for the Year 1983-84*', Tribal Development Department, Manipur, p. 5.
78. *Ibid.*, p. 9.

79. '*Annual Administrative Report for the Year 1984-85*', Tribal Development Department, Manipur, p. 2.
80. *Ibid.*, p. 5.
81. *Ibid.*, 1985-86, p. 1.
82. *Ibid.*, 1986-87, p. 1.
83. *Ibid.*, 1986-87, p. 1.
84. The Government of Manipur, Secretariat, *Tribal Development Department, Order by the Governor of Manipur, Imphal*, the 25th November, 1988.
85. *Ibid.*, dated, 15th December, 1988.
86. *Ibid.*, dated, 20th December, 1988.
87. *Ibid.*, dated, 28th February, 1989.
88. *Ibid.*, dated, the 7th March, 1989.
89. *Ibid*, dated, 7th March, 1989.

CHAPTER-III

The Governor and the Legislature

The head of a State in a federation is an integral part of the State legislature. In the United States, the Governor of a State is regarded as an important part of the State Legislature. In India also, the Governor in a State forms a very important integral part of the State legislature. The State legislature in India consists of the Governor and the Legislative Assembly if there is unicameral system of legislature. But in those States where there is bicameral legislature, the State legislature, consists of the Governor, the Legislative Assembly and the Legislative Council as provided by Article 168 of the Constitution of India. It means that the institution of the Governor in a State is a very important part of the State legislature. Any bill passed by the Legislative Assembly and Legislative Council cannot become an Act without the signature of the Governor. The relationship between the Governor and the State legislature may be examined under the following heads.

Nomination of Member

Under Articles 171(3)(e) and (5) of the Constitution of India, the Governor of a State in India has the power to nominate one-sixth of the members to the Legislative Council, having special knowledge in literature, science, arts, social science, Co-operative movement, etc. Further, according to Article 333 of the Constitution of India, if the Governor thinks that representation of the Anglo-Indian community is required, he can nominate one member to the

Legislative Assembly. Here one question arises, i.e., whether the Governor is bound to accept the advice of the Chief Minister in the nomination of members or not? The Constitution is silent in this regard. From the practical experience of the working of Indian political system it seems that there is no hard and fast rule to consult the Chief Minister or the Council of Ministers. For example, "Shri Prakash, the Governor of Madras in 1952 admitted that he did not consult the Council of Ministers when he nominated Gopalachari".[1] Or as a gesture, the Governor may consult the Chief Minister in nominating the members to the Legislative Council. Regarding this matter the practice followed from time to time and from State to State in the working of the Indian Political System is not uniform. It depends on the concerned Governor to consult or not to consult the Chief Minister in the nomination of member in the legislature and also is depended with the personality of the Governor.

Summoning the Legislative Assembly

According to Article 174(1) of the Constitution, the Governor has the right to summon the Houses or each House of the State legislature from time to time but six months should not intervene between its last sitting in one session and the date appointed for its first sitting in the next session. Ordinarily the State legislature is summoned on the advice of the Chief Minister or Council of Ministers. But after 1967, when some of the Chief Ministers lost the confidence of the House, they were not prepared to summon the Assemblies. They wanted to take advantage of this article which says that the gap between the last sitting in the previous session and the first sitting in the next session should not be more than six months. Some of the Governors wanted the Chief Ministers to face the Assembly without undue delay whereas some Governors completely ignored the defections that took place and allowed the minority government to stay in office. For example "in West Bengal, the Governor Dharam Vira asked the Chief Minister to face the Assembly in 1967. When the Chief Minister did not agree to accept the advice of the Governor he was dismissed.[2] The same happened in Punjab in 1970 and in Orissa in 1971. On the other hand, Governor K.K. Reddy in Madhya Pradesh, in 1967, Ananthasayanam Ayyangar in Bihar in 1968 and B. Gopal Reddy in UP in 1969, etc., did not ask their Chief Ministers to summon the Assembly to prove their majority.

In the States having bicameral legislature, the Governor within the constitutional framework can use his discretion to summon the joint sitting of the two Houses. There is also a convention that the Governor summons the session of both the Houses of the legislature simultaneously after every general election. But the convention of summoning the joint session of the Houses is not followed when the lower house is not in existence because of its dissolution.

One important question is whether the Governor is bound to accept the advice of the Chief Minister in summoning the legislature? It becomes more complicated when the Chief Minister enjoys majority support in the House. Another question is whether the Governor can insist upon the Chief Minister to alter the date for summoning the House fixed by the Cabinet? Regarding these questions, there are varied opinions. K. Santhanam expressed: "The Governor will be entitled to call the session if he thinks that the Ministry is trying to evade its responsibilities under the Constitution"[3] Dr. L.M. Singh also had the similar view and said, "If and when there is a reason to believe that the Chief Minister and the Council of Ministers do not command the support of a clear majority in Legislative Assembly, the Governor can in his discretion take steps to ascertain the position".[4] A.K. Chand opines that "the function of the Governor is to act on the advice of the Chief Minister".[5] The Law Ministry held that "the Governor has no power to summon the State Legislative Assembly against the wishes of the Chief Minister". Here the Chief Ministers leading coalition governments in the States generally adopted delaying practice by bypassing the Assembly sitting and at the same time they also did not advise the Governor to call the session of the Assembly when they have doubt of majority support in their respective Legislative Assemblies. The Committee of the

Governors set up in 1971 by the then President V.V. Giri was of the view that "whenever the Chief Minister is asked by the Governor to summon the session in order to prove his majority, the Chief Minister should call the session of the Assembly within the shortest possible time. The Committee further suggests that if the Chief Minister falls to comply with the advice of the Governor, the latter should install an alternative Ministry in the State".[6]

Proroguing the Legislative Assembly

It is only the Governor to whom the Constitution vests the power to prorogue the House or Houses of the State legislature under Article 174(2)(a). The Governor's action in the prorogation is unquestionable on any ground. D.D. Basu in his book *Commentary on the Constitution of India* states: "This function is non-justiciable".[7] Prorogation of the Assembly is an important function of the Governor as it brings an end to the session of the Assembly.

The Governor can prorogue the Assembly from time to time. His power to prorogue "may be exercised while the House stands adjourned under orders of the Speaker. Adjournment of the House is an executive power of the Speaker of the Assembly giving interruption in the course of one and the same session. The order of the Governor to prorogue the Assembly takes effect as soon as it is notified in the official Gazette, notwithstanding anything in the Rules of the House of the country".[8] From this it is clear that after the Speaker had adjourned the Assembly, the Governor can prorogue the Assembly again by an order notified in the official Gazette.

One important question regarding the prorogation of the Assembly is: Does the Governor always act on the advice of the Chief Minister? Generally, the Governors prorogue the State Assemblies on the advice of the Chief Ministers. For example in 1967, K.C. Reddy, the Governor of Madhya Pradesh prorogued the Legislative Assembly on the advice of the Chief Minister, D.P. Mishra. The Governor at a Press Conference said: "He prorogued the session of the Vidhan Sabha for the present in view of the political developments in the State particularly during the last few days and in the interest of the proper functioning of democracy".[9] The then Union Minister, Y.B. Chavan supported the action of the Governor by saying that "the Governor of the State acted constitutionally on the advice of the Chief Minister".[10] The same was done "in Uttar Pradesh in January 1968 when the Governor prorogued the State Assembly on the advice of the Chief Minister, Charan Singh while the strength of the S.V.D. was reduced to minority due to the withdrawal of the S.S.P. and CPM on account of the crisis for leadership in the State".[11]

In proroguing the Legislative Assembly, the Governor may also be guided by the advice of the Speaker. The Governor of Punjab, D.C. Pavate in his book, *My Days as Governor* expressed: "I took nearly ten days to consider these issues. When I found that there were several instances of this kind in our country to support the Speaker, I prorogued the House on April 10, 1970. This was how Sardar Badal was put in the saddle by the parties concerned as head of an Akali-Jan Sangh Coalition Government".[12] Really the Governor of Punjab prorogued the Legislative Assembly while the resolution for the removal of the Speaker was there. The Governor said, "he was satisfied that the notice for the removal of the Speaker was received after the prorogation of the Assembly. So he was entitled to ignore it".[13] Again in Tamil Nadu in 1972 the Governor K.K. Shah prorogued the Legislative Assembly on the advice of the State Chief Minister although the notice for the removal of the speaker was pending for further consideration.

In all the above cases, the Governor acted on the advice of the Chief Minister and the Speaker. The latter two were always together in all cases.

On the other hand, there were also instances where the Governor was not guided by the advice of the Chief Minister. In 1967, the Governor of West Bengal, Dharam Vira asked the Chief Minister to face the Assembly immediately, instead of proroguing, and when the Chief Minister refused to do so, he was dismissed. The action of the Governor was very much criticized by pointing out that the Governor behaved in a partisan manner.

From all these, we may conclude that the Governor should exercise this prorogation power on a justiciable ground when the Legislative Assembly is in session. "The former M.P. Pitambar Das was of the opinion that, 'the Chief Minister's advice for prorogation is not binding on the Assembly only after his own judgment".[14] Of course the Chief Minister has a right to request the Governor for prorogation. But the Governor may ignore this right (1) when, the Assembly is in session; (2) when it is facing a major crisis; and (3) when there is no-confidence motion against the Ministry or Speaker. The Governor may not accept the advice of the Chief Minister to prorogue the House during the budget session.

Dissolution of the Legislative Assembly

Besides summoning and proroguing the Assembly, the Governor has an important power of dissolving the Assembly under Article 174(2)(b). Ordinarily the life span of the State Legislative Assembly is 5 years. But the Governor under the said Article can dissolve it earlier. "According to K.V. Rao, the interpretation of dissolution of Assembly may be in two directions, i.e., (i) a normal dissolution envisaged under Article 174(2)(b); and (ii) dissolution leading to emergency".[15] The first type of dissolution is normal dissolution of the Assembly after the completion of its term of 5 years. And the second type of dissolution may take place during the life of the Assembly, i.e., before the completion of its term. On the recommendation of the Governor, President's Rule is imposed and the Governor as an agent of the Centre rules over the State.

The important question to examine is whether the Governor is bound to accept the advice of the Chief Minister in the dissolution of the Assembly or not? The Administrative Reforms Commission dealt the dissolution of a Legislative Assembly in its report on Centre-State relations. In para 18 of the Report, it is stated that "Article 174(2)(b) of the Constitution empowers the Governor to dissolve the Legislative Assembly. The dissolution of the Assembly may be on the recommendation of the outgoing Chief Minister or in special circumstances at the discretion of the Governor. In the former case, the Governor should exercise his discretion in deciding whether or not he should accept the recommendation of the Chief Minister for dissolution of the Assembly".[16] The concluding part of the Report states that "if the recommendation for the dissolution is made with a view to obtaining the verdict of the electorates on a major policy issue on which the outgoing Ministry has suffered defeat, the Governor should accept the advice of the outgoing Chief Minister. In other cases, the Governor should use his discretion to decide whether he should accept the advice of the Chief Minister or not".[17] On the other hand, according to Dr. Pavate:

> "a Governor has absolute power to dissolve a Legislative Assembly under Article 174(2)(b) in certain situation. There is no trouble if after dissolving the house he also orders elections within two or three months and asks his Ministry to continue in office as a Caretaker Government till the elections are over".[18]

The controversy about the exercise of a Governor's power to dissolve a Legislative Assembly has been considered time and again by the Union Government and now no consensus has been arrived at. Of course, there is unanimity of opinion at least among Governors that if a Chief Minister who has not lost his majority advises dissolution after losing majority, whether to accept his advice or not, will depend on the circumstances. "If a Chief Minister advises dissolution to seek a fresh mandate on a matter of major policy even after defeat, the Governor must accept the advice".[19]

After the fourth General Elections of 1967, in India in the multi party coalition governments, the Governors seem to be more powerful than the Chief Ministers. "In July 1967, Madhya Pradesh Chief Minister, D.P. Mishra requested the Governor to dissolve the Assembly. The Governor did not oblige him. Instead the Governor allowed G.N. Singh, the leader of the Samjukta Vidhayak Dal to form the Ministry".[20] Similarly "in Orissa, Chief Minister R.N. Singh Deo recommended to the Governor, Dr. S.S.

Ansari for the dissolution of the Assembly in 1971. The Governor accepted his resignation but rejected his advice to dissolve the Assembly".[21]

The action of the Governor to dissolve the Assembly or not is also influenced by the party politics of the Central Government and the State Government. As such there is no uniformity in exercising the power to dissolve the Assembly by the Governor.

Address to the Legislative Assembly

The normal function of the Governor under Article 176(1) of the Constitution of India is to address the Legislative Assembly at the commencement of the first session after each general election. In the case of a State having a legislative council, both houses assembled together and the Governor shall inform the legislature of the cause of its summon. This is the constitutional duty of the Governor. In the address, the Governor mentions the performance of the Government in the last year and the policies and programmes in the coming year.

Sometimes it is not possible for the Governor to read out the address from top to bottom. For example, "in 1969, the Governor of Andhra Pradesh Khandubhai Desai was not allowed to read out his address by the agitated members of the House who were leading the Telengana Movement. The annoyed Governor left the House keeping the address on the table".[22] In the same year, the Governor of West Bengal Dharma Vira skipped a portion of the prepared address though the atmosphere in the House was quite peaceful. Here the Governor willingly left out some portion of the Address. Contrary to this, "the Governor of Punjab, P.C. Pavate read out the full text of the address to the joint session of the legislature without omitting portions which were regarded critical of his own actions".[23]

The Address is generally prepared by the Ministry. Whether the Governor has the right to omit any part of it or not is still controversial.

Opposition walk out and creation of bad atmosphere by the members of the House when the Governor reads out his address largely depends on the prevailing political atmosphere of the State. For example "in Tamil Nadu in January 1980, the members belonging to DMK, Congress(I), Forward Block and Muslim League boycotted the Governor's address in a joint session of the Legislative Assembly and Legislative Council as the Government has lost the right to govern after the ruling party's defeat in the recent Lok Sabha election".[24] Language may also be one of the causes for boycotting the Governor's address. "In 1968 in Punjab during the Chief Ministership of Sardar Gill, the Governor Pavate read out the address in a joint sitting of both Houses in Punjabi. The opposition led by Sardar Gurnam Singh boycotted the address. Then the Governor switched from Punjabi to English. A Samyukta Socialist member again asked the Governor to read the speech in Hindi".[25] Thus because of language, the members boycotted the address of the Governor. The Governor has also to administer the oath or affirmation according to the Second Schedule of the Constitution of India to the newly elected MLAs.

Issuing of Ordinances

The Governor has the power to issue ordinances when the State Legislature is not in session. If the Governor is satisfied that a particular law is immediately needed, he may issue an ordinance. The ordinance so promulgated cease to operate at the expiration of six weeks from the reassembly of the Legislature or earlier, if a resolution disapproving such an ordinance is passed by the Legislative Assembly and agreed by the Legislative Council, if any. Ordinarily these ordinances are issued by the Governor on the advice of the Chief Minister. Some Governors refused to do so when they were convinced that it would amount to political corruption. "P.C. Pavate, Governor of Punjab refused to issue an ordinance which would have enabled the legislators to hold certain offices of profit in 1970. He thought that it was nothing but political corruption and violation of his oath of office. In U.P. also, the Governor G.D. Tapase refused to issue an ordinance recommended by the Chief Minister for the nationalization of private homoeopathic colleges".[26]

For certain matters, however, the Governor cannot issue an ordinance without the permission of the President. They are:

(a) If a Bill containing the same provisions would have required the previous sanction of the President for introduction into the legislature.
(b) If the Governor would have reserved a Bill containing the same provisions for the President.
(c) If an act of the State Legislature containing the same provisions would have been invalid without the assent of the President.

It means that the Governor can issue an ordinance mainly in respect of those matters which are in the State List. The ordinance issued by the Governor will lapse if not approved by the State Legislature at the expiration of six weeks from the reassembly of the legislature.

If the ordinance is not approved by both Houses of the State Legislature or by the Legislative Assembly if it is a uni-cemeral, then it will cease to operate. But in most cases, the legislature approved the ordinances promulgated by the Governor.

Assenting to Bills

A bill passed by the State legislature cannot became an Act without the assent of the Governor. After a bill is passed by the State legislature, it is presented to the Governor for his assent under Article 200 of the Constitution. The Governor may take one of the following three courses:

(a) he may give his assent,
(b) he may withhold his assent and return it for reconsideration unless it is Money Bill, and
(c) he may reserve it for the consideration of the President under Article 201 of the Constitution.

If the Governor withheld his assent to a bill, it is sent for reconsideration to the House with suggestions. The House will reconsider it in the light of the suggestions made by the Governor. The House may pass it with or without the recommendations suggested by the Governor. In such cases, the Governor may either give his assent or reserve it for the consideration of the President.

Under Article 200 and 254(2) of the Constitution of India, it is the constitutional duty of the Governor to reserve any bill which affect the powers and position of the High Court and if connected with subjects enumerated in the concurrent list.

Sending Message to the Legislature

The Governor may send message to the House or Houses on a Bill pending in the Legislature or otherwise. The House shall consider any matter required by the message to be taken into consideration. Thus the Governor by way of sending message to the Legislature can make suggestions regarding any bill.

MANIPUR

The institution cf the Governor and its relation with the legislature in Manipur can be traced back to 1963 when "Manipur was placed under the Union Territories Act 1963. The head of the State under this Act was called Administrator. The Administrator, from time to time had the power to summon, prorogue and dissolve the Assembly".[27] The Administrator also had the right to address and send messages to the Legislative Assembly with respect to a Bill then pending in the Assembly or otherwise. The Assembly considered any matter required by the message to be taken into consideration. The Administrator had to administer an oath or affirmation according to the form set up for the purposes in the First Schedule to every member of the Legislative Assembly without the previous sanction of the Administrator, if such Bill or amendment makes provision with respect to any of the following matters, namely:

(a) Constitution and organization of the Court of the Judicial Commissioner.

(b) Jurisdiction and powers of the Court of the Judicial Commissioner with respect to any of the matters in the State List or the Concurrent List in the Seventh Schedule to the Constitution.

Certain financial bill or amendment relating to the imposition, abolition, remission, etc., of any tax, the appropriation, and the expenditure and the receipt of moneys out of the Consolidated Fund of the Union Territory could not be introduced into or moved in the Legislative Assembly except on the recommendations of the Administrator.

Under the North-Eastern Areas (Reorganistion) Act 1971, Manipur was headed by a Governor like all other States of India. The relation between the Governor and the legislature may be examined under the following heads:

Nomination of Member

There is only one House in the Legislature of Manipur, i.e., the Legislative Assembly. So the question of nomination of members to the Legislative Council does not arise. However, the Administrator under the Union Territories Act 1963 had the power to nominate 2 women members to the Legislative Assembly of Manipur. But this power to nominate members was not given into the hands of the Governor when Manipur was granted full statehood in 1972.

Summoning the Legislative Assembly

The Governor of Manipur like the Governors of other State "has the power to summon the Legislative Assembly. The Assembly shall be summoned by the Governor from time to time to meet at such time and place as he may appoint".[28] Generally the summoning of the Legislative Assembly by the Governor was done according to the advice of the Chief Minister. On the advice of the Chief Minister, the Governor usually summons the Legislative Assembly by observing the constitutional norm that the gap between the last sitting in the previous session and the first sitting in the next session should not be more than six months. In Manipur, there was no cases of conflict between the Governor and the Chief Minister in summoning the Legislative Assembly. "Conflict between the Governor and the Chief Minister in summoning the Legislative Assembly usually loses his majority support in the Assembly. In Manipur most of the ministerial crisis occurred during the session of the Assembly".[29] Of course, political maneuvering and political bargaining started before the session (i.e., during the gap of 6 months) of the Legislative Assembly. In 1973 and 1974, the Chief Minister Md. Alimuddin might have wanted to avoid the summoning of the Legislative Assembly as he was sure of losing majority support in the Assembly. But the Governor L.P. Singh had to observe the constitutional provision. So the Chief Minister, Alimuddin had to resign during the session of the Assembly both in 1973 and 1974. The same happened in 1977. After the formation of Janata Government at the Centre, most of the Congress MLAs defected to the Janata Party. It may be remembered that the Congress Ministry headed by R.K. Dorendro Singh had a comfortable majority of more than 50 members in the House. More Congress MLAs resigned from Congress and joined the Janata. Here also, the Chief Minister, R.K. Dorendro Singh was almost sure that he was going to lose the Ministry if summoned the Assembly. But he could not go against the wishes of the Governor L.P. Singh to summon the Legislative Assembly. Both the Governor and the Chief Minister had to observe the Constitutional provision of summoning the Legislative Assembly within six months from the date of the last sitting. "During the session of the Legislative Assembly in May 1977, the Chief Minister, R.K. Dorendro Singh lost the majority support and resigned his ministry on 13 May, 1977".[30] Thus the Governor always observed the constitutional provision of summoning the Legislative Assembly from time to time, sometimes ignoring the desire or wishes of the Chief Minister.

Proroguing the Legislative Assembly

The Governor of Manipur prorogues the Legislative Assembly from time to time under Article 174(2)(a) of the Constitution of India. In the prorogation of the Assembly, the Governor may be guided by the advice of the Chief Minister and the Speaker. "When the Assembly is prorogued, all pending notices shall lapse and fresh notices shall be given for the next session. But the questions, the bills, any business, any motion, resolution or amendment, etc., which had been entered in the list of business but were postponed and remained pending for answer at the close of the proceeding session shall not lapse".[31]

In Manipur, the Governor very rarely exercised this power of prorogation. In the prorogation of the Assembly so far from 1972 onwards there is no conflict between the Governor and the Chief Minister.

Dissolution of Legislative Assembly

The Governor of Manipur has the power to dissolve the Legislative Assembly under Article 174(2)(B) of the Constitution of India. The Governor exercised both the two types of dissolution, i.e., normal dissolution and dissolution leading to emergency. The Governor of Manipur exercised the power of normal dissolution in 1979. The Legislative Assembly formed after the General Assembly elections of 1974 was able to complete its term of 5 years through the politics of Manipur was characterized by defections, instabilities of Ministries, etc. There were as many as five different Ministries during this period. The Governor had to exercise his power of normal dissolution of the Legislative Assembly in 1984 again when the Assembly was formed after the General Assembly Election of 1980 completed its full term of 5 years. The same can be said of the dissolution of Manipur Legislative Assembly by the Governor in 1989.

The Governor of Manipur had to exercise his power of dissolution leading to emergency only once during the long period of 18 years, i.e., from 1972 to 1990. That was in March 1973, when the MPP lead coalition Ministry under the Chief Ministership of Md. Alimuddin was reduced to a minority. Nine members including 2 Ministers and the Deputy Speaker of the MPP led ULP Ministry defected to the opposition on 15 March, 1973. The strength to the ruling party was reduced to 26 only and that of the opposition was 32. One MLA remained natural and one seat was vacant following the death of a ULP member. The Chief Minister, Md. Alimuddin submitted the resignation of his Ministry to the Governor on 26 March, 1973. The Congress led Progressive Democratic Alliance met the Governor and requested him to allow them to form the Government. The Governor observed the growing political situation and the scale of defection very minutely. It may also be remembered that "the Congress was also the ruling party at the Centre under the Prime Ministership of Indira Gandhi. But the Governor, L.P. Singh exercised his power of dissolution of Assembly leading to emergency. Accordingly, President's Rule was imposed in Manipur on 28 March, 1973 and the State Assembly was dissolved".[32] Here we may say that the Governor has acted either on the advice of the outgoing Chief Minister, Md. Alimuddin or on his own judgment.

Address to the Legislative Assembly

The Governor of Manipur exercised the normal function of addressing the Legislative Assembly under Article 176(1) of the Constitution of India. "At the commencement of the first session after each general election to the Legislative Assembly and at the commencement of the first session of each address the House as required by Article 176 of the Constitution".[33] After the delivery of the speech by the Governor, the Speaker reports to the House that the Governor had been pleased to make a speech and lay a copy of the speech on the table. "The House is at liberty to discuss the matters referred to in such address on a Motion of Thanks moved by a member and recorded by another member".[34] The address having been adopted with or without amendment shall be presented to the Governor by the Speaker in such manner as may be prescribed. The Speaker shall report to the House the Governor's reply, if any, to the Motion of Thanks but if the House is not sitting, the reply shall be communicated to the Members of the House. The Speaker usually allot time for the discussion of the matters referred to in the Governor's Address to the House under Article 175(1) of the Constitution.

Just after getting statehood in 1972, the Governor B.K. Nehru in his address to the Legislative Assembly on 30th March, 1972 expressed, "it is historical in the sense that this session marks the beginning of a new chapter of full statehood which the people of Manipur have not acquired in full measure of equality with the people of other States in our great country of India".[35] The Governor cutlines the future programmes to be taken by the newly formed MPP led coalition Government under the Chief Ministership of Md. Alimuddin, much as "the establishment of Board of Secondary Education, taking over of Adim Jati Technical Institute by the Government. In the field of higher education and culture, the Governor mentioned the establishment of Jawaharlal Nehru University Centre at Imphal, State Kala Akademy, etc".[36] The Governor L.P. Singh in his address to the Legislative Assembly on March 26, 1974 the various programmes undertaken by the MPP led coalition government led by Chief Minister, Md. Alimuddin. In addition to the achievements, "the Government is also taking up actions for further development in the field of agriculture, Planning and development of the hill areas, industries, culture, services, forest, medical, etc."[37] There were "two amendments on the Motion of Thanks to the Governor's Address proposed by K. Shyam Singh and M. Meghachandra Singh both opposition members. The address was discussed thoroughly for 2 days, i.e., 28th and 29th March, 1974 by the members of the Assembly and at last put to vote by the Speaker regarding the Amendment motion".[38] The two amendments were lost. Thus every year from 1975 onwards, the Governor of Manipur delivered his address on the first day of the session of the Manipur Legislative Assembly. "When Sayed Muzaffar Husain Burney became the

Governor, the members of the Legislative Assembly were addressed for the first time in Manipuri language".[39] He continued to do so during his term, i.e., upto 1984. "The address delivered by General K.V. Krishna Rao (Rtd.) during his term of Governorship from 1985 to 1989 mentioned the various programmes undertaken and to be undertaken by the Government when the United Front Ministry led by the MPP under the Chief Ministership of R.K. Ranbir came to power, the Governor Chintamani Panigrahi in his address delivered in 1990 outlined the various programmes to be taken up by the Government".[40]

The only occasion where the members of the Assembly boycotted the Governor's address was in 1979. On the first day of the budget session, the Governor "L.P. Singh delivered his address on the opening day of the budget session. Opposition members belonging to the Congress(I) and the CPI boycotted the Governor's address as a protest against the failure of the Government in maintaining the law and order and fulfilling the minimum aspirations of the masses".[41] It may be remembered that very shortly the Janata Ministry under the Chief Ministership of Yangmaso Shaiza was dismissed by a Presidential Order issued under Article 356 of the Constitution on 14 November, 1979.

Administration of Oath

After every Assembly elections, the Governor of Manipur administered the oath to every newly elected member of the Legislative Assembly. This result in establishing a close relationship between the Governor and the members of the Legislative Assembly.

Issuing of Ordinances

The Governor of Manipur has the power to issue Ordinances when the State Legislature is not in session. The issuing of Ordinance by the Governor of Manipur started from January 1975. "On 20th January, 1975, the Governor, L.P. Singh issued two Ordinances namely, the Manipur Legislature (Removal of Disqualification) (Amendment) Ordinance 1975 and the Manipur Land Revenue and Land Reforms (Miscellaneous Amendment) Ordinance".[42] These two Ordinances were issued by the Governor mainly on the advice of the Chief Minister, R.K. Dorendro Singh, who was heading Congress ULP coalition government. These Ordinances were placed at the next session of the Assembly for approval. The legislature duly approved these ordinances. Two more ordinances were issued by the Governor in the same year. In 1976, the largest number of Ordinances, i.e., 5 were issued by the Governor L.P. Singh. They were the Departmentalisation of Union Accounts (Transfer of Personnel) Ordinance, the Manipur Co-operative Societies Ordinance, the Manipur Land Revenue Land Reforms (Validation of Proceedings) Ordinances, the Manipur Agricultural Credit Operation and Miscellaneous Provision (Banks) Ordinance and the Metal Corporation (Nationalization and Miscellaneous Provisions) Ordinance. These Ordinances were issued when R.K. Dorendro Singh was the Chief Minister of the Congress-CPI coalition government. During his Chief Ministership one more Ordinance was promulgated by Governor, L.P. Singh. "During the time of Janata Ministry headed by Yangmaso Shaiza, Governor L.P. Singh issued as many as seven Ordinances, i.e., 2 in 1977, 3 in 1978 and 2 in 1979. Perhaps the Governor felt it necessary to promulgate these Ordinances because of their importance. One such Ordinances being the Manipur Panchayati Raj (Second Amendment) Ordinance 1979 issued on 10 November, 1979".[43] When the Congress(I) came to power in 1980, the Governor L.P. Singh continued to issue three more Ordinances. When S.M. Burney became the Governor of Manipur in August 1981, he promulgated as many as 7 Ordinances, one in 1981, two in 1982 and four in 1983. All these were during the Chief Ministership of Rishang Keishing heading pure Congress(I) Ministry. There was also no problem of disapproving these ordinances as the Congress enjoyed majority in the Assembly.

From October 1983 upto the present day, no Ordinance has been issued although there were three Governors. They are S.M. Burney, General K.V. Krishna Rao and Chintamani Panigrahi.

As we know, the largest number of Ordinances were issued by Governor L.P. Singh during his term from 1973 to 1981.

Assenting to Bills

A bill passed by the Manipur Legislative Assembly become an Act with the assent of the Governor. "A copy of every bill introduced in the House shall, immediately after its introduction, be forwarded by the Secretary to the Governor and the President for their information".[44] Thus the Governor of Manipur is always in touch with every bill introduced in the Legislative Assembly.

Most of the bills passed by the Manipur Legislative Assembly during the period from 1972 to 1990 got the assent of the Governor, thereby becoming an Act. Sometimes the Governor returned a bill for reconsideration by the House. "When a bill which has been passed is returned by the Governor to the House, for reconsideration, the point or points referred for consideration or the amendments recommended in his message shall be put before the House by the Speaker, and shall be discussed and voted upon in the same manner as amendments to a bill or in such other manner as the Speaker may deem proper for their consideration by the House".[45] There are also times when the Governor of Manipur reserves a bill for the consideration of the President. For example, the controversial Manipur Official Language Bill was reserved by Governor L.P. Singh for the consideration of the President in 1978. The bill became an Act only after getting the assent of the President.

The assent of the Governor is also very much necessary to a bill relating to the hill areas of Manipur. In fact, the Governor is the final authority for enacting a bill into a law on matters relating to Hill areas of Manipur. The Governor has always to protect the interest of the hill areas "when a Bill as reported by the Hill Areas Committee is not passed by the House in the form in which it has been reported but is passed in a form, which in the opinion of the Speaker, is substantially different from that as reported by the Hill Areas Committee or is rejected by the House, the Speaker shall submit to the Governor".[46] When a Bill is not approved by the

Hill Areas Committee but is passed by the House, the Speaker shall submit to the Governor the bill as passed by the House together with the report of the Hill Areas Committee. Thus the Legislative Assembly of Manipur has no power to enact a law on matters relating to the hill areas without the approval of the Governor.

Sending Message to the Legislature

The Governor of Manipur has also the power to send message to the Legislative Assembly under Article 175(2) of the Constitution. The Speaker shall read the message to the House and give necessary directions in regard to the procedures that shall be followed for the consideration of matters referred to in the message.

Thus the relations between the Governor and the Legislative Assembly of Manipur is very close. Of course, the close relationship is maintained through the Speaker. "The Governor can communicate to the House by a written message delivered by the Speaker or through a minister. Communications from the Assembly to the Governor is generally made by formal address, after a motion is made and carried in the House or through the Speaker. The Speaker informs all the proceedings of the Assembly daily to the Governor".[47,48,49]

References

1. *The Modern Review,* Calcutta, Vol. LXXXIV, IV, 2 August, 1953, p. 18.
2. Siwach, J.R., *Dynamics of Indian Government and Politics*, Sterling Publishers Pvt. Ltd., New Delhi, 1985, p. 133.
3. *The Statesman* (Delhi), 11.11.1967.
4. *Ibid.*
5. *The Statesman* (Delhi), 12.11.1988.
6. Presidential Secretariat, "the Report of the Governor, New Delhi, 1967, p. 45.
7. Basu. D.D. *Commentary on the Constitution of India*, S.C. Sarkar & sons (P) Ltd., Calcutta, 1967, p. 291.
8. Basu, D.D., *Shorter Constitution of India*, Prentice Hall of India Pvt. Ltd., New Delhi, 1984, p. 370.

9. *The Times of India* (New Delhi), 22.7.1987.
10. *Ibid.*
11. *The Hindustan Times* (New Delhi), 1.11.1968.
12. Pavate, P.C. *My Days as Governor*, Vikas Publishing House, New Delhi, 1974, p. 137.
13. *The Hindustan Times*, 12.4.1970.
14. *Organiser*, New Delhi, Vol. 12, 1968, p. 5.
15. *The Journal of Society for Study of State Government*, Varanasi, Vol. IV, No. 364, 1911, p. 368.
16. Report of the Administration Reform Commission on Centre State Relations, New Delhi, 1967, p. 46.
17. *Ibid.*
18. Pavate, P.C. *op. cit.*, p. 203.
19. *Ibid.*
20. *The National Herald*, 23.7.1967.
21. *The Hindustan Times*, (New Delhi), 1.11.1971.
22. *The Hindustan Times*, (New Delhi), 15.8.1967.
23. *The Statesman*, 15.3.1967.
24. *The Times of India*, 1.2.1981.
25. Pavate, P.C., *op. cit.*, p. 43.
26. Siwatch, J.R., *op. cit.*, p. 135.
27. The Government of Union Territories Act 1963, Section 6(1)(2).
28. *Rule of Procedure and Conduct of Business*, Manipur Legislative Assembly Secretariat, Imphal, 1988, 5th edn. p. 6.
29. Assembly Proceedings, Manipur Legislative Assembly 1973-1977.
30. Assembly Proceedings, Manipur Legislative Assembly, May, 1977.
31. Rule of Procedure and Conduct of Business, Manipur Legislative Secretariat, Imphal, 1988, 5th edn., p. 12.
32. Ksh. Bimola Devi, Government and Politics in Manipur, 1950-1990, an unpublished. Ph.D. thesis submitted to Guahati University, 1981, p. 164.
33. Rule of Procedure and Conduct of Business, Manipur Legislature, Imphal, 1988, 5th edn., p. 14.
34. *Ibid.*
35. Manipur Legislative Assembly Secretariat, Compilation of Governor's Addresses, 1972-1987, Imphal, p. 1.
36. *Ibid.*
37. Manipur Legislative Assembly Secretariat, Compilation of Governor's Addresses, 1972-1987, Imphal, p. 1.
38. Assembly Proceedings Manipur Legislative Assembly, 1974, p. 67.

39. Manipur Legislative Assembly Secretariat, Compilation of Governor's Address, 1972-1987, p. 124.
40. Assembly Proceeding, Manipur Legislative Assembly, Imphal, February 1990.
41. The *Amrita Bazar Pratika*, 20.3.1979.
42. Government of Manipur (Law Department), Ordinance, Imphal, 1984.
43. *Ibid.*
44. Rules of Procedure and Conduct of Business, Manipur Assembly Secretariat, Imphal, 1988, p. 55.
45. *Ibid.*, p. 63.
46. *Ibid.*, p. 62.
47. Interview with Dr. H. Borbabu Singh, Speaker, Manipur Legislative Assembly. 3.8.1990.
48. Interview with Md Helaluddin, Ex-MLA, Ex-Cabinet Minister. 2.5.1990.
49. Interview with Dr. Nimaichand Luwang, MLA, Ex-State Minister, 31.5.1950.

CHAPTER-IV

The Governor and the Council of Ministers

In every State or in every form of government, there is a group of elected people, big or small, to aid and advice the head of the state in running the administration. In England where there is monarchical form of government for giving aid and advice to the King. In U.S.A. and U.S.S.R. also, there are a group of people, Cabinet or Council of Ministers to aid and advise the head of the state. In an authoritarian regime also, we found the existence of the Council of Ministers. For example in Pakistan in spite of the dictatorial rule of Yahya Khan and General Zia-ul-Haq, there was small group of people known as Cabinet. The President consulted them in all matters of administration. In Spain and Brazil, the Council of Ministers play a very important role in giving aid and advice to the head of states.

The Constitution of India emphasizes the important role of the Council of Ministers in the political system of India. The real executive is the Council of Ministers. Article 74 of Constitution of India provides that there shall be a Council of Ministers with Prime Minister at the head to aid and advise the President in the exercise of his functions. "The President appoints the Prime Minister and other Ministers are appointed by the President on the advice of the Prime Minister".[1] The advice tendered by the Minister to the President cannot be enquired into in any court. For the smooth functioning of administration, the relation between the President and the Council of Ministers should always be cordial.

Likewise in the States, the Constitution of India provides that "there shall be a Council of Ministers with the Chief Minister at the head to aid and advise the Governor in the exercise of his functions except so far as he is by and under the Constitution required to act in his discretion".[2] There is a close relation between the Governor and the Council of Ministers. The Minister hold office during the pleasure of the Governor. Before entering his office, the Governor administers the oath of office and secrecy to the Minister according to the prescribed form in the Third Schedule.

The relation between the Governor and Council of Ministers may be examined under the following heads.

The Governor and the Appointment of the Chief Minister

The Chief Minister is appointed by the Governor. The leader of majority party in the Lower House, i.e., Legislative Assembly is usually appointed as Chief Minister. The choice is obvious when there is one leader of a single party commanding majority in the Legislative Assembly. When there is no party commanding majority, the Governor has to exercise his discretion in appointing the Chief Minister. Here the choice or the appointment of the Chief Minister is not an easy one. The Governor has to observe the political trend and situation in the State very minutely. His main objective is of course to form a government or to appoint a Chief Minister who will be able to form a stable government. When there are more than one person claiming leadership to form the Government, the Governor, sometimes has to verify the number as well as the physical support of the concerned MLAs. The Governor may call upon the leader and his MLAs at his Residence. He can talk to leader and the MLAs and try to know the degree of their loyalty to the leader and the genuineness of their support. Then the Governor can form his own opinion and can invite the leader whom, he thinks, will be able to command majority support in the Legislative Assembly and thereby ensuring the political stability in the State.

The Governor and the Appointment of the Council of Ministers

According to the Constitution of India, "it is the Governor who appoints the Council of Ministers with the Chief Minister at the head to aid and advise him in the exercise of his functions except in matters where the Governor acts in his discretion."[3] It is the discretion of the Governor to take final decision in the appointment of the members of the Council of Ministers. Of course, it is the Chief Minister of the State to select and submit the list of the member of the Council of Ministers to the Governor for appointment. Usually the Governor accepts and appoints the member as submitted by the Chief Minister. Sometimes the Governor may exercise his discretion in the appointment. His decision is final and the validity of such a decision cannot be questioned in a court of law. On the other hand, the appointment of the member of the Council of Ministers by the Governor means that he has the power to discuss any member of the Council of Ministers at any time. Really it is the Chief Minister who will approach the Governor for the dismissal of any member of the Council of Ministers. Here also the Governor may exercise his discretion by not dismissing the concerned Minister if he thinks that there is no valid ground for the dismissal. The Chief Minister cannot do anything in this regard. The decision of the Governor is final. The Governor can act, in particular cases in his discretion. Practically the Ministers hold office during the pleasure of the Chief Minister. But there are times when the pleasure of the Governor has become more important than the pleasure of the Chief Minister. This happened in U.P. in 1970 in Charan Singh's case. "In U.P. Governor, G.D. Tapase did not accept the advice of Ram Naresh Yadav for the dismissal of his Ministers owing allegiance to RSS"[4].

The Governor and the Size of the Council of Ministers

The Constitution of India does not provide any fixed size of the Council of Ministers. It is for the Chief Minister to determine the size of the Council of Ministers. The role of the Chief Minister in determining the size of the Council of Ministers is very important because under Article 164(1) of the Constitution he is the head of the Council of Ministers and all the Ministers are appointed by the Governor on his recommendation. The Chief Minister select his own team and distributes portfolios. The Governor has a little say regarding the size of the Council of Ministers. He has to accept the size of the Council of Ministers as determined by the Chief Minister.

The Chief Minister is, however, guided by several factors in determining the size of the Council of Ministers. First, the position of the Chief Minister in the party is important. If the Chief Minister is a tourring personality in the party, he will have a comparatively free hand. Second, if the Chief Minister happens to be a person whose leadership is under challenge, then his hand will be very tight. During the time of the Congress rule in both the Centre and the State in the early 1970s and 1980s, the size of the Council of Ministers has to be approved by the Congress High Command. The Chief Minister had a minimum say in this regard. Third, the strength of the ruling party in the Assembly is also a factor. If the ruling party has a narrow majority in the Assembly, the Chief Minister has to satisfy the various factional leaders, thereby affecting the size of the Council of Ministers. Fourth, in the case of the coalition government the choice of the Chief Minister is very limited. The Chief Minister, first of all, has to allot seats to the various coalition partners. The concerned parties nominate their candidates in the Ministry. The Chief Minister has no say in their selection. He merely forwards their names to the Governor for their appointment. The members are the nominees of the coalition parties and not of the Chief Minister. The Governor simply accepts the list as recommended by the Chief Minister.

It has been very often criticized that the size of the Council of Ministers is unduly large and it heavily burdens the exchequers. The necessities of a welfare state incredibly expand the functions of government and as a result the number of government departments is increased. It is for the responsible government to see that all departments are headed by a political chief to see the proper implementation of policy and be answerable to the legislature for its work. But unduly large Ministry has now become the norm in all States. It is more so in the case of smaller States. The condition of limiting the size of the Council of Ministers to 10 or 11 per cent of the total number of seats of the Legislative Assembly has not been observed. The tendency is to increase the size of the Council of Ministers in order to satisfy the various aspirations of many persons or parties. In this regard, the Governor has nothing to do but to accept the recommendations of the Chief Minister.

Relation between the Governor and the Chief Minister

One of the most important constitutional powers of the Governor is to appoint the Chief Minister according to Article 164(1) of the Constitution of India. The Governor has to exercise this power after every Assembly election or whenever there is mid-term vacancy in the office of the Chief Minister when there is clear majority of a party in the Assembly, the Governor has no difficulty in the appointment of the Chief Minister. The difficulty arises when none of the political parties enjoys clear majority in the Assembly. Generally, the Governor invite the leader of the largest single party to form the government. It is only after his refusal that the Governor can invite the leaders of other parties to form the government. This practice was usually followed in the sixties, seventies and early eighties with few exceptions.

The Governors are appointed by the President on the recommendation of the Prime Minister. In the fifties and upto the middle of sixties, a convention has developed where the concerned Chief Ministers were consulted before the appointment of the Governors. This practice was there when the Congress party ruled at both the Centre as well as the States. But after the 1967 elections, this practice was not followed. For example Dharam Vira was appointed the Governor of West Bengal against the wishes of the Chief Minister. The same happened in Haryana when B.N. Chakravarti was appointed Governor of the State. The Constitution provides "that it shall be the duty of the Chief Minister to communicate to the Governor all decisions of the Council of Ministers relating to administration of the affairs of the State and proposals for legislation"[5]. He may also "call for such other informations relating to administration of the affairs of the State and proposals for legislation as he may deem necessary"[6]. He can direct the Chief Minister to "submit to the consideration of the Council of Ministers any matter on which a decision has been taken by a Minister but which has not been considered by the Council of Ministers"[7]. Once the matter so referred is approved by the Council of Ministers it becomes binding on the Governor. The Governor cannot reopen any decision already taken by the Council of Ministers.

The cordial relationship between the Governor and the Chief Minister is very much necessary for the smooth working of the State government. The Governor, though a constitutional head of the State, in certain situations can play an important part not only in the appointment of the Chief Minister but can also help him remaining in office by summoning, proroguing and dissolving the Assembly according to recommendation of the Chief Minister. If there is strain relationship between the Governor and the Chief Minister, many problems may develop and there may not be stability in the office of the Governor as well as in the office of the Chief Minister. For example in 1968, Ajoy Mukherjee, the Chief Minister of West Bengal forced the Central Government to withdraw Dharma Vira from the State. Because the Governor had dismissed him as Chief Minister in 1967. On the other hand, there may also be cases where in spite of the cordial relationship between the Governor and the Chief Minister, the term of office of the Governor may be affected. In 1980, the Tamil Nadu Governor Prabhu Das Patwari was dismissed on this ground. In 1981 also Raghukul Tilak, the Governor of Rajasthan was dismissed on similar charge. If the Chief Minister belonged to the party in power at the Centre, the Governor has been allowed to continue in office after the completion of his term. In 1973, B.N. Chakravarti, the Governor of Haryana, continued in office for more than three years on daily wages"[8]. B.D. Tapase, the Governor of Haryana and B.D.

Sharma, the Governor of Madhya Pradesh also continued for about a year on daily wages.

Thus the relationship between the Governor and the Chief Minister cannot be examined completely if one does not take into account the attitude and the role of the ruling party at the Centre. The relationship is influenced in many ways by the attitude and role of the party in power. The Governor and the Chief Minister has to understand fully the national politics and the politics of the ruling power at the Centre.

The Governor and Other Members of the Council of Ministers

The Constitution of India does not provide any direct relationship between the Governor and other Ministers. The Constitution only says that there shall be a Council of Ministers with the Chief Minister at the head to aid and advise the Governor in the exercise of his functions. The Chief Minister acts as a link between the Governor and other members of the Council of Ministers. For a successful democratic system, joint responsibility is very much necessary. The Minister (Council of Ministers) is one and indivisible. A Minister differing from the policy determined by the Council of Ministers must resign from the government. The Governor cannot dismiss the Council of Ministers as a body as long as it enjoys the confidence of the Legislative Assembly. But on the advice of the Chief Minister, an individual Minister may be dismissed by the Governor. Ministers hold office during the pleasure of the Governor. Constitutional propriety also demand that the Minister should immediately resign when a hint is given by the Chief Minister. Thus theoretically an individual Minister cannot approach the Governor regarding any policy matter of the Government. The Governor, on the other hand, is not supposed to hear and accept any view or advice given by an individual Minister. The relation between the Governor and the Council of Ministers is guided by the principle of joint responsibility and joint action.

But in our country, it is not unusual to find a Minister differing from the decision of the Council of Ministers. The differences among the Ministers and some Ministers on the one hand and the Chief Minister on the other are very frequent.

It has become a normal feature rather than an exception in the working of democratic system in India. Further in most of the States, there has been a rift between the party President and the Chief Minister. When Ministers contradict each other, they plague ministerial solidarity, demoralize services and paralyse the governmental machinery. In such situations, the Ministers can meet the Governor individually and tender advice. "The question whether any, and if so, what advice was tendered by Ministers to the Governor cannot be inquired into by any court"[9]. Ministerial advice, as such cannot be brought before courts. Indirectly it means that the relations between the Governor and his Ministers are confidential.

The norm of parliamentary democracy, i.e., the Council of Ministers always working as a team, is not always followed in India. The prevailing political situations and atmosphere very much influenced the working of the Council of Ministers and also the relation between the Governor and the Council of Ministers as a whole.

MANIPUR

The Council of Ministers played a very important role in the administration of Manipur since the rule of the King, i.e., from 33 AD to 1709, the King remained strictly a constitutional ruler. "The Council of Ministers could assist and advice the King"[10]. At the same time, the Council could accept or reject the proposals of the King. From 1709 onwards, the King tried to assert his real authority. Thus depending on situations and circumstances, the King became a constitutional as well as the real head of the State. One noteworthy feature of the system was that the members of the Council of Ministers, i.e., *Mantries* represented the thirty two divisions of the State. During the period from 1891 to 1947, the members of the *Darbar* did not exercise any important role in the administration as the State was under the control of the British.

After Independence of India, Manipur was integrated into the Indian Union on 15 October, 1947. With the application of the Merged States (Laws) Act 1949, the administration of Manipur was taken over by a Chief Commissioner and placed as a Part C State under the Constitution of India. During the period from 1950 to 1063 there was no Council of Ministers in the real sense of the term. The Chief Commissioner was not a nominal but real head of the State.

The Territorial Council of Manipur was converted into the Territorial Assembly on July 1963. A small Council of Minister was formed with M. Koirang Singh, the Chief Minister as its leader. The relation between the Lt. Governor and the Council of Ministers from 1967 to 1969 was characterized by cordial relationship between the Lt. Governor and Chief Minister on one hand and the Lt. Governor and other members of the Council of Ministers on the other. The Council of Ministers during the period was also a homogeneous one.

The real Council of Ministers enjoying powers came into existence in March 1972 after the Assembly elections, the first one after getting statehood by Manipur. The relation between the Governor and the Council of Ministers from 1972 onwards may be examined as follows:

The Governor and the Appointment of the Chief Minister

In the elections to the Legislative Assembly of 1972, no party secured majority. The Congress secured the largest number of seats, i.e., 16. The Manipur People Party secured 15 seats. It was somewhat difficult for the Governor B.K. Nehru to invite a person to form the Government. The general impression was that the Governor will invite the leader of the Congress(I) Party to form the ministry as the Party was the single largest party. It may also be remembered that the Congress(I) was also the ruling party at the Centre. On the other hand, Alimuddin, the leader of the United Legislature Party, requested the Governor to allow him to form the Government. He was able to collect as many as 32 members, i.e., 15 MPP, 3 SSP, 1 Congress(O) and 13 Independent. After observing the political situation and political development, the Governor had to invite Alimuddin, as the Chief Minister of the State. After the downfall of the Ministry, on the recommendation of the Governor, President Rule was imposed in Manipur on 28 March, 1973. Here the action of the Governor was very much criticised on the ground that he could have invited the leader of the Progressive Democratic Alliance, having 31 members to form the Government or the Governor could at least meet and talk the leader of the Alliance and could examine whether a stable Ministry is possible or not? After the mid-term election of 1974, both the MPP and the Congress tried to win over different groups and independents in order to form the Government. This time, the MPP was the single largest party. The leaders of both the Congress and the MPP requested the Governor to invite them to form the Government. The Governor ultimately invited Alimuddin to form the Ministry. Here the "Governor has to act according to the desire of the electorate as shown by the results of the Assembly elections. Alimuddin formed the government under the name of United Legislature Party on 4th March, 1974"[11]. Due to defections, the ministry falls on 8th July, 1974. Progressive Democratic Front comprising MLAs of Congress, CPI, MHU (Shaiza Group) and Manipur Democratic Party (formed by those MLAs defected from ULP) elected Yangmaso Shaiza as their leader. The Governor, L.P. Singh had to act according to the changing political situation of the State, thereby inviting Yangmaso Shaiza to form the Ministry. The Governor had to observe the changing political situation very minutely and carefully as ministerial instability characterized the politics of the State. "Due to a rift between Chief Minister Shaiza and the Congress nominees in the Ministry, nineteen MLAs of Manipur Democratic Party joined the Congress"[12]. The Governor, L.P. Singh had to observe these situations and finally he had to invite R.K. Dorendro Singh, the leader of the Congress ULP coalition to form the government. After about seven months, the Chief Minister, R.K. Dorendro Singh requested the Governor to allow him to form a pure Congress ministry. The Governor advised him to resign first. Accordingly, R.K. Dorendro Singh tendered the resignation of his D.L.P. ministry on 23rd July, 1975. On the same day, the Governor appointed R.K. Dorendro Singh as Chief Minister of Manipur for a second time as the head of the Congress, CPI coalition Government. In June 1977, the Governor, L.P. Singh had to appoint Yangmaso Shaiza, an M.P. be the Chief Minister of the State. This was due to the changed political scenario of India as a whole. Most of the existing MLAs had defected to the Janata Party and the strength of the party had increased to more than 50. The Congress Party which had 57 members immediately before the Lok Sabha election had not a single Congress MLA in the Assembly when Shaiza's party commanded more than 50 members in the House, the Governor had no alternative but to appoint him as Chief Minister of the State. After the Assembly elections of January 1980, the Governor, L.P. Singh appointed the leader of the largest single party [Congress(I)] R.K. Dorendro Singh as the Chief Minister on 14th January, 1980. Very shortly, this coalition ministry falls on 27th February, 1981 due to defection of 11 members to the opposition. Again on 19 June, 1981, the Governor appointed Rishang Keishing of the Congress(I) to head a coalition ministry. The desire of the Governor, it seems was only to see that a popular ministry was formed in order to promote the welfare of the people. In August 1986, the Congress(I) Ministry headed by Rishang Keishing submitted its resignation from the ministry. The Council of Ministers could not work as a team due to the politics of dissension among the members of the Council of Ministers. Because of this, the Central High Command of the ruling Congress party instructed the Governor, Gen. K.V. Krishna Rao, to appoint R.K. Jaichandra Singh, a Union Minister of State as Chief Minister of the State in order to solve the crisis within the Council of Ministers. It may be noted that Rishang Keishing was enjoying majority support in the Council of Ministers as well as in the Legislative Assembly of the State. Here the Governor acted more on the direction of the Central High Command than any other norm of Parliamentary democracy. After the Assembly elections of February 1990, no political party secured majority to form the ministry. The Congress(I) secured the largest number of seats, i.e., 26 in the House of 60. On the other hand, opposition parties like M.P.P. and Janata Dal secured 10/10 each. The two parties along with other parties formed United Front and requested the Governor, Chintamani Panigrahi to allow them to form the government. "The leader of Congress(I), R.K. Dorendro Singh also requested Governor to invite him to form the Ministry by giving him some time"[13]. The United Front claimed the support of 32 members. "The Governor, Chintamani Panigrahi, at last, invited to form the ministry"[14]. Here the action of the Governor was also partly influenced by the change at the Central level, i.e., National Front ministry at the Centre.

The Governor and the Appointment of Members of Council of Ministers

Normally the Governor appoints the persons recommended by the Chief Minister to be the members of the Council of Ministers. In January 1972, after getting statehood, the Chief Minister recommended 12 persons to be appointed as members of the Council of Ministers. The Governor, B.K. Nehru simply accepted the list and appointed them as ministers. In March 1974 also, the Chief Minister, Alimuddin recommended the names of 12 persons to be appointed as members of the Council of Ministers. There was also certain controversy regarding a section of Manipur Hill Union led by Yangmaso Shaiza joining the ULP ministry. The Governor was in full knowledge of these developments and controversies. But the Governor did not express a single word. He simply appointed the persons recommended by the Chief Minister as members of the Council of Ministers. In July 1974, when Yangmaso Shaiza became the Chief Minister, he recommended nine persons to be appointed as members of the Council of Ministers. The Governor B.K. Nehru appointed these persons as members of the Council of Ministers. Later on a conflict developed between the Chief Minister, Shaiza and the Congress nominees in the Ministry regarding the appointment of the Congress nominees to the Council of Ministers. "Yangmaso Shaiza, the Chief Minister did not accept the nominees of the Congressmen"[15]. The Governor did not interfere into these conflicts. He simply remained as a silent observer. On 6 December, 1974, R.K. Dorendro Singh, the leader of the Congress ULP coalition under the name of Democratic Legislature Party requested the Governor L.P. Singh to appoint only one State Minister as member of the Council of Ministers on the day of the swearing-in-ceremony. Accordingly the Governor appointed M. Gouramani Singh and sworn as State Minister. Later on, the Chief Minister recommended the names of 17 persons to be appointed as members of the Council of Ministers. The Governor accepted the recommendation and appointed them as Ministers. The same happened in July 1975 when R.K. Dorendro Singh was again sworn in as the head of Congress-CPI coalition government. The Chief Minister recommended only four persons namely Rishang Keishing, R.K. Ranabir, T.P. Kiulongpao and S. Bijoy to be appointed as Cabinet Ministers. The Governor appointed these four persons as Cabinet Ministers. "The Governor, L.P. Singh advised the Chief Minister to appoint at least one from the CPI in the Council of Ministers"[16]. The Chief Minister recommended the name of the M. Meghachandra Singh, CPI to appoint as Cabinet Minister. Thus the Governor sometimes advised the Chief Minister in the appointment of members of Council of Minister in the appointment of members of Council of Ministers in order to maintain stability in the ministry. When the Janata Ministry under the Chief Ministership of Yangmaso Shaiza was installed on 29 June, 1977, only one Cabinet minister namely Alimuddin was sworn in as a Cabinet Minister. He was appointed by the Governor, L.P. Singh on the recommendation of the Chief Minister. Later on more ministers were appointed by the Governor on the recommendation of the Chief Minister. When R.K. Dorendro Singh was appointed as the Chief Minister of the coalition Government in January 1980, only two persons namely Rishang Keishing and Ngurdinglien were appointed by the Governor as Cabinet Ministers. The Council of Ministers was expanded in two phases, i.e., first on 20 February, 1980 and second on 11 June, 1980 so as to include more members in "the Council of Ministers in order to get representation from different partners of the Ministry"[17]. The selection of members from different political partners to be appointed as members of the Council of Ministers was done by the concerned political parties in consultation with the Chief Minister. The Governor simply appointed those persons recommended by the Chief Minister. The same happened in June 1981 when Rishang Keishing was appointed as Chief Minister of the coalition Ministry. On the swearing-in-ceremony as many as seven persons were sworn as members of the Council of Ministers. The Governor appointed them on the recommendation of the Chief Minister. In 1984, the task for the appointment of ministers were somewhat simpler on the part of the Governor and the Chief Minister as the Ministry was purely Congress one. The selection of members of the Council of Ministers was confined only to one political party. The Governor accepted the recommendation of the Chief Minister without any reservation. In February 1990, the Governor, Chintamani Panigrahi appointed R.K. Ranabir Singh as the Chief Minister of the United Front Ministry. On the recommendation of the Chief Minister, "another four ministers (three Cabinet Ministers and one State Minister) were also appointed and sworn on 23rd February, 1990"[18]. One MLA namely N. Ibomcha Singh was expected to be appointed by the Governor and sworn as minister on the same day. Everything was ready for him. But at last his name was not in the list recommended by the Chief Minister. That was why the Governor did not appoint him as minister. Later on, the Chief Minister clarified that N. Ibomcha Singh was not the approved nominee of the Congress(S), a partner of the United Front. Minister has no power to recommend a person to be a member of the Council of Ministers. The matter lies within that political partner to recommend a person to be a minister. There also, of course, conflicts between the organizational front and the legislative front plays a very important part in the selection process. The Governor, though officially, has the power to appoint a minister. But really he is always bound to act according to the recommendations made by the Chief Minister.

The Governor and the Size of the Council of Ministers

For small States like Manipur, the size of the Council of Ministers is a very important aspect of the working of the political system. There are only 60 members in the Legislative Assembly of Manipur. So if Manipur follows the Parliamentary convention of limiting the size of the Council of Ministers to 10 per cent or 11 per cent of the strength of the Legislative Assembly, the Council of Ministers should not exceed more than six or seven members. But the size of the Council of Ministers is always bigger than what is prescribed by the convention of parliamentary democracy. The first Council of Ministers after getting statehood in 1972 consisted of more than 10 members, i.e., 12 (5 Cabinet, 4 State Ministers and 3 Deputy Ministers). The Governor B.K. Nehru had nothing to say regarding the size of the council of Ministers. He simply approved the size as submitted by the Chief Minister. The size of the Council of Ministers in the second MPP led ULP Ministry was the same, i.e., 12 as compared with the one formed by the first MPP led ULP Ministry. However the number of Cabinet Ministers increased to 8, the numbers of State Ministers reduced to 3 and there was only one Deputy Minister. The size of the Council of Ministers of the Progressive Democratic Front Ministry, 1974 headed by Yangmaso Shaiza was smaller as compared with the Council of Ministers of 1972 and the second one of March 1974. There were only 4 Cabinet Ministers, 5 State Ministers and one Deputy Minister. Of course, the size was supposed to be expanded to include members from the Congress(I). The Governor, L.P. Singh did not interfere into the matter regarding the size of the Council of Ministers. It was entirely left into the hands of the Chief Minister to determine the size of the Council of Ministers. Another example was the Council of Ministers of Congress ULP coalition government, (December 1974 to July 1975) headed by R.K. Dorendro Singh. The size was extra-ordinary consisting of 19 members (8 Cabinet Ministers, 9 State Ministers and 2 Deputy Ministers). It seems that the Chief Minister tried to include more members representing different sections of the Congress and ULP. The Governor approved the action taken by the Chief Minister. In the Congress-CPI coalition Government of July 1975, the size of the Council of Ministers was smaller as compared with the last one. It consisted of only 6 Cabinet Minister, and 9 State Ministers. There were no Deputy Ministers in this Council. In the Janata Ministry of June 1977, headed by Yangmaso Shaiza, the Council of Ministers was small at first, consisting of only 3 Cabinet Ministers and 5 State Ministers. Later on, of course, the Ministry was expanded to include more cabinet ministers and other categories of ministers. The size of the Council of Ministers headed by R.K. Dorendro Singh in January 1980 was also quite big consisting of 6 Cabinet Ministers, 11 State Ministers. The ministry was coalition one consisting of Congress(U), MPP, KNA and Independents. One thing, we may note is that the size of the Council of Ministers of coalition government is always bigger than the one formed by one political party. As pointed out, the Governor generally did not interfere in determining the size of the Council of Ministers. It is the Chief Minister, who determines the size of the Council of Ministers. Another notable example was the Council of Ministers formed after the Assembly elections of February 1990. "At the swearing-in-ceremony only 5 ministers (4 Cabinet Ministers and 1 State Minister) was sworn in"[19]. In the second phase, the Council of Ministers was expanded including 18 more Ministers. There are 15 Cabinet Ministers and 8 State Ministers. "It may be noted that the United Front Ministry headed by R.K. Ranabir Singh has the support of only 32 members"[20]. The Chief Minister was also criticized by the local papers and public for the large size of the Council of Ministers. But next day two more State Ministers were added to the Council of Ministers, thereby resulting the Council to have 25 members. It was for the first time in the political history of Manipur that the Council of Ministers consists of more than 20 members, i.e., 25. Here opinions were also expressed mentioning the name of the Governor. That is the Governor should advise the Chief Minister to limit the size of the Council of Ministers. But the Governor, Chintamani Panigrahi remained as a silent observer and simply approved the size given by the Chief Minister. It was also somewhat difficult on the part of the Chief Minister. R.K. Ranabir Singh, as the Government is a coalition one consisting of MPP, Congress(S), Janata Dal, MNP and CPI. There is still the demand to include 2 more ministers representing the hill areas Ukhrul and Chandel districts of Manipur. But now, it is constitutionally or theoretically reduced to 9 since the 1st January 2004, 91st Amendment Act of the Constitution of India mentioning 15 per cent downsizing of Ministry mainly in order to strengthening antidefection. Practically the size of the Council of Ministers is always larger than other States of India if we take into account the strength of the Legislative Assembly. Manipur, though small, consists of various ethnic groups. The Chief Minister is determining the size of the Council of Ministers has to take into consideration the representation of the ethnic groups, districts and parties, if the Ministry is a coalition one. In fact the total number of Cabinet Ministers at present is 12 including Chief Minister and one more Chairperson of Hill Area Development Committee.

The Governor and the Chief Minister

The relation between the Governor and the Chief Minister in Manipur is always guided by the provisions of the Constitution of India. According to Article 164(1) of the Constitution of India, the Governor always appoints the Chief Minister after every Assembly elections. During the period from 1972 to 1977, no political party secured majority in the Legislative Assembly. It was, therefore, somewhat difficult on the part of the Governor to appoint Chief Minister. But the Governor was always guided by the principle of maintaining political stability in the State in appointing a Chief Minister. Regarding the appointment of the Governor, the convention of consulting the Chief Minister is sometimes followed. But in most cases, the Chief Ministers of Manipur since 1972 onwards always accepted the Governors appointed by the President. There was no conflict of any kind between the Governor and the Chief Minister regarding the appointment of the former. From 1972, (the year in which Manipur got statehood) to the present day, the

Chief Ministers of Manipur did not express any open comment regarding the appointment of the Governor.

According to the Constitution of India it is the duty of the Chief Minister to communicate to the Governor all decisions of the Council of Ministers relating to administration of the affairs of the State and proposals for legislation. Accordingly the Chief Minister of Manipur informed the Governor all decisions of the Council of Ministers. The advice given by the Governor to the Chief Minister is always considered to be very important in taking a decision and in reviewing it. The Chief Minister of Manipur also informed the Governor about any proposal for legislation. For example, the Chief Minister, R.K. Dorendro Singh informed the Governor L.P. Singh about the proposal for legislating the controversial Manipur Official Language Bill 1978. After him, Chief Minister of the Janata Government Yangmaso Shaiza always sought the advice of the Governor regarding the passing of the Manipur Official Language Bill. "It was only in March 1978 that the Manipur Assembly unanimously passed the Manipur Official Language Bill 1978"[21]. It may be said that the Governor L.P. Singh was instrumental in passing the Manipur Official Language Bill. It was also possible because of the cordial relationship between the Governor and the Chief Minister. Sometimes due to political situation and circumstances, the relation between the Governor and the Chief Minister may become strained. For example in 1979, there was strong demand from the opposition parties [Congress(I) and CPI] to dismiss the Janata ministry headed by Yangmaso Shaiza. "They boycotted the Governors address on the opening day of the budget session as a protest against the failure of the government in maintaining the law and order and fulfilling the minimum aspirations of the masses"[22]. According to the Chief Minister, Shaiza, there was no constitutional crisis in the State and the administration was running smoothly. After observing the political situation and development, the Governor, L.P. Singh had to take the undesirable step of dismissing the Janata Ministry. "The Governor in his report has drawn attention to the deteriorating law and order situation in Manipur and said the administration had been rendered increasingly ineffective in dealing with the activities of extremists because of gross maladministration, favouritism and nepotism"[23]. There are also times when the Central Government intervened into the relationship between the Governor and the Chief Minister, if the ruling party at both the Centre and the State is the same. During 1986-1987, the relationship between the Governor General (retired) K.V. Krishna Rao and the Chief Minister Rishang Keishing was characterized by the dissident politics of 3 senior Cabinet Ministers. Practically the Council of Ministers was divided into 2 groups, one led by the Chief Minister and the other led by the three Cabinet Ministers. On the other hand, the ruling party, the Congress enjoys majority in the State Assembly. The dissident group became very strong demanding a change in the leadership of the Chief Minister, Rishang Keishing. The group also levelled many charges of corruption and bribery against the Chief Minister. The Governor at his own level tried to solve the problem many times but failed. At last, the Central High Command of the Congress party intervened and forced Rishang Keishing to resign from the Chief Ministership and appointed R.K. Jaichandra Singh, a Union Minister of State as Chief Minister of the State. On the advice of the Governor, a senior Cabinet Minister and a leader of the dissident group, I. Tompok Singh was appointed as Home Minister of the State. Later on the relationship between the Chief Minister and the Home Minister became very strained. "The Chief Minister went to the extent of requesting the Governor to dismiss the Home Minister while the latter was at New Delhi"[24]. Here the Governor General (Retired) K.V. Krishna Rao acted judiciously. He did not accept the request of the Chief Minister. But advised him to have cordial relationship with the Home Minister, thereby maintaining political stability in the State. Here the Governor play a very important and useful role in the politics of the State.

The Governor and Other Ministers

Although the Constitution does not provide any direct relationship between the Governors and other ministers, it does not mean that there is no relationship between the Governor and other ministers. Because the Governor is the final authority to appoint and to dismiss the ministers. Manipur being a very small State, the Governor knows every Minister personally and cordially. There is always good and cordial relationship between the Governor and individual minister. The relation between the Governor and individual minister has become important when there is conflict between the Chief Minister and an individual Minister. From 1972 to 1981, there was no major conflict between the Chief Minister and the Ministers. As such the relation between the Governor and the individual Minister was also good and cordial. It may be remembered that during the period from 1972 to 1977, the politics of Manipur was characterized by political instability. In spite of this, the different Chief Ministers during the period was able to take all the Ministers along with him in matters relating to the administration of the State. It also seems that the individual Ministers were more interested in their own personal political benefits and positions than any political principle or issue of the State.

But from the early part of 1980s, the Governor played a very important role in maintaining political stability as well as in resolving the conflict between the Chief Minister and his senior cabinet ministers. In the middle of 1980s there developed a major conflict between the Chief Minister, Rishang Keishing and three of his senior cabinet colleagues, i.e., I. Tompok Singh, Education Minister, L. Lalit Singh, Finance Minister and Soso Lorho, P.W.D. Minister. Later on these three Cabinet Ministers formed a group within the Council of Ministers known as dissident group. This dissident group became a very strong force even paralyzing the functioning of the government. In these circumstances, the Governor directly discussed with the concerned ministers in order to resolve the crisis. I. Tompok Singh the dissident leader expressed: "The Governor had played his card very correctly. My impression of Governor was very good"[25]. And to other Ministers, the Governor has no role to play in resolving the ministerial crisis. "The Governor is not involved in the dissident politics. It was the crisis in the Congress(I) Party"[26]. Another former Cabinet Minister said, "No conflict brought to the Governor. All ministerial crisis are settled by the Chief Minister"[27]. Thus to the ministers who are not concerned with dissident politics, the Governor has nothing to do. And to the minister, who was very much active in the dissident politics, the Governor played a very important role.

Regarding the working of the department headed by a Minister, there is no direct kink between the Governor and the concerned Minister. But the Governor can call the file of a concerned department and generally no change or amendment is done by the Governor. When a question is asked: can a Minister directly approach the Governor regarding any matter affecting his department, the answer is yes, but not always. "The opinion expressed by the Governor may not be binding on the Minister"[28]. In case of a conflict among the Ministers, the Governor can play a constructive role in resolving the crises, as it happened in Manipur during the period 1985 to 1987. But the Governor may fail if the Ministers have taken their respective political stand on their differences.

During the Chief Ministership of R.K. Jaichandra Singh (1988 to 1989), the Governor General (Retired) K.V. Krishna Rao played a very important role in resolving the crisis between the Chief Minister and some senior Cabinet colleagues. The Governor even went to the extent of not accepting the recommendation of the Chief Minister to dismiss the Home Minister, I. Tompok Singh, the Governor always acted in such a manner to maintain political stability and proper functioning of the government.

Thus there is no direct relationship between the Governor and other Ministers. The relationship is mainly channelled through the Cabinet Minister. But practically it seems that the Governor has direct relationship with the Ministers if the political situation of the State requires it. Here the Governor, in most cases acted as a friend, guide and philosopher of the Chief Minister and other Ministers of the State.

References

1. Article 75(1), The Constitution of India.
2. Article 163(1), The Constitution of India.
3. Article 163(2), The Constitution of India.
4. Siwach, J.R., *Dynamics of Indian Government and Politics*, Sterling Publisher, New Delhi, 1985, p. 131.
5. Article 167(a), Constitution of India .
6. Article 167(b), *ibid.*
7. Article 167(c), *ibid.*
8. Siwach, J.R., *op. cit.*, p. 145.
9. Article 163(3), The Constitution of India.
10. Ksh. Bimola Devi, "Government and Politics in Manipur 1950-1980", an unpublished Ph.D. Thesis submitted to Gauhati University, 1981, p. 28
11. Th. Gokul Singh, Defection in Manipur, 1963-1977 Imphal, 1978, p. 18.
12. Government of Manipur, *Annual Administrative Report, Imphal, 1974-1975*, p. 10.
13. *Poknapham* (local daily), 23-2-1990.
14. *Huyen Lanpao* (local daily), 24-02-1990.
15. Th. Gokul Singh, *op. cit.*, p. 52.
16. In accordance with the advice given by the Governor to co-opt the CPI in the ruling party in view of the unsteadiness of the numbers, the Congress sought the co-operation of C.P.I.
17. Ksh. Bimola Devi, *op. cit.*, p. 180.
18. *Huyen Lalpao*, 24-02-1990.
19. *Huyen Lalpao* (local daily), 24-02-1990.
20. *Ibid.*, 04-03-1990.
21. Ksh. Bimola Devi, *op. cit.*, p. 311.
22. The *Amrita Bazar Patrika*, 20-03-1979.
23. *Ibid.*, 15-11-1979.
24. *Huyen Lalpao* (local daily). 05-11-1988.
25. Interview with I. Tompok Singh, former Education and Home Minister, 20-01-1990.
26. Interview with Dr. Nimaichand Luwung, former State Minister, P.W.D., 31-05-1990.
27. Interview with Md. Helokiddin, former Cabinet Minister, Fishery, 01-05-1990.
28. Interview with I. Tompok Singh, former Education and Home Minister, 20-01-1990.

CHAPTER-V

Discretionary Power of the Governor

The Oxford English Dictionary gives three meanings of discretionary power, i.e., (1) at one's sense of fitness, (2) as one thinks fit, and (3) at his mercy. Generally by discretionary power we mean the power exercised at the individual judgment of a person as he thinks fit.

The concept of discretionary power in India can be traced back to the Government of India Act 1935. 'The British Governor was required to act in his discretion in dealing with the special responsibilities of the province'.[1]

Background

The makers of the Constitution of India provided in a memorandum submitted to the Provincial Constitution that "the Governor would be aided and advised by his Council of Ministers in the exercise of his functions. And the Governor would exercise his discretion in the following matters:

(i) the prevention of any grave menace to the peace and tranquillity of the province or any part thereof;
(ii) the summoning and dissolving of the provincial legislature;
(iii) the Superintendence, direction and control of selections; and
(iv) the appointment of the Chairman and the members of the Provincial Public Service Commission and of the Provincial Auditor General."[2]

The proposals of the Provincial Constitution committee was approved by the Constituent Assembly and were incorporated in the Draft Constitution. The Draft Constitution specified the discretionary power of the Governor. The Governor was required to observe the instructions issued to him for the use of his discretionary power. When the Draft Constitution was discussed in the Constituent Assembly, there were two sections. One section was in favour of deletion of discretionary power of the Governor. H.V. Kamath said, 'when the President of India was made bound to accept the advice of the Council of Ministers in the exercise of all his functions why the Governor was given certain discretionary power in the exercise of his functions'.[3] Rohni Kumar Chaudhury held the view that the Governor would not be a mere symbol in the State when he was being allowed to act in his discretion. He said, "If the Governor was given the power to act in his discretion, there would be no power on earth to prevent him from becoming an arbitrary ruler".[4] The other section wanted to retain the discretionary power of the Governor. T.T. Krishnamachari, Mahavir Tyagi and Alladi Krishna Swamy highly favoured in the discretionary power of the Governor. Keeping in view the political situation of the country, Brajeshwar Prasad suggested that the Governor should be vested with the power to act in his individual judgement.[5] Mahavir Tyagi opined that the discretionary power of the Governor was essential for maintaining the link between the Centre and the States. After hearing different opinions, Dr. Ambedkar, the Chairman, concluded, "I have no doubt in my mind that the retention in or vesting the Governor with certain discretionary powers, is in no sense contrary to or in no sense a negation to the responsible Government".[6] Thus the Draft Article 146(1), in *status quo*, was accepted by the Constituent Assembly. It later became Article 163(1) of the Constitution of India.

Discretionary Power in the Constitution of India

Nowhere in the Constitution of India except Article 163(1) mentions the discretionary power of the Governor. And Article

159 of the Constitution indirectly gives the discretionary power to the Governor. While preserving, protecting and defending the Constitution and law of the country, the Governor can exercise his discretion according to particular situations. This was supported by scholars like Prof. M.V. Pyles. One reason for not inserting discretionary power in the Constitution could be that the framers wanted it to develop as a convention. T.T. Krishnamachari said, 'it would be entirely unnecessary and superfluous to give such discretion in the Constitution which really should arise out of conventions that grow up from time to time.'[7] According to Dr. Iqbal Narain, the Governor's discretion may be underlined into two parts. First, the discretion mentioned in the Constitution, i.e., the Constitutional discretion; and second, the hidden discretion which may be derived from exigencies of the political situation. It may be styled as situational discretion.[8] We may say that under the Constitution of India, the Governor possess discretionary power. Article 163(2) may be interpreted in such a way that it contains both the constitutional discretion and the situational discretion. The exercise of situational discretion by the Governor became common in India especially after the 1967 General Elections when the Congress failed to capture power in some States. In exercising the situational discretion, the Governor is not bound by the advice of the Council of Ministers.

Generally the Governor can exercise his discretion in the following matters, i.e., (i) Appointment of a Chief Minister (ii) Dismissal of a Chief Minister/Ministry, (iii) Summoning of the State Legislative Assembly, (iv) Dissolution of the State Legislature, (v) In getting or seeking of information from the Chief Minister on both the legislative and administrative matters, (vi) In giving assent to the Bills passed by the State legislature or in returning the Bills, (vii) Reservation of Bills for the consideration to the President, (viii) Promulgation of Ordinances, (ix) Reporting to the President regarding the breakdown of Constitutional machinery in the State under Article 356, (x) In exercising the special power given under the Sixth Schedule of the Constitution of India, and (xi) To exercise the power under Article 371 of the Constitution of India.

Appointment of Chief Minister

When a political party secures clear majority in the Legislative Assembly after the General Election, the Governor has no discretion. He has to appoint the leader of the majority party as the Chief Minister of the State. But when there is no single political party securing absolute majority in the Assembly, the task of the Governor becomes a bit difficult. Before inviting the leader of the coalition or combined parties, the Governor has to watch and observe the political atmosphere of the State. His task becomes a bit easier if a particular combination of political parties which formed coalition Government, before the election is returned with a clear majority. The recognized leader of such a united front or coalition should be invited by the Government.[9] The difficult task of the Governor is when there is no single political party or a combination of parties with a clear majority in the Assembly. In such a situation, the discretionary power of the Governor has great importance in the appointment of the Chief Minister.

Normally the Governor invites the leader of the single largest party to be the Chief Minister. If he is not in a position to form the Government, the Governor normally invites the leader of the second largest party to form the Government. Before inviting, the Governor has to examine whether the said leader has the capacity to command a working majority or not. Side by side the Governor has to take greatest care in grasping the personality cult of the political leaders. In Bihar, just after the mid-term election of March 1969, the Governor invited Harihar Singh, the leader of the largest single party, i.e., the Congress to form the Ministry.[10] But when the non-Congress parties emerged as the single largest party in the State Assemblies in the beginning of 1970s, the exercise of the discretionary power by the Governor seemed to be in a different direction. For example, in Bengal after the mid-term election of 1971, the United Leftist Front led by the CPI(M) has secured 123 seats out of 280, thus emerging as the single largest party. But the Governor invited Ajoy Kumar Mukherjee, the leader of the newly organised Democratic Coalition to form the Government.[11] Again the Governor of Orissa in 1971 called upon Biswanath Das, the leader of the Orissa United Front ignoring the claim of the Congress(R), the single largest party to form the government.[12] However in 1971, the report of the Governor's Committee headed by Bhagawan Sahay, the Governor of Jammu and Kashmir suggested that the leader of the single largest party may be invited to head a government. But the leader of the largest party has no absolute right 'to claim that he should be asked to form the government. The relevant test is not the size of a party but the ability to command the support of the majority in the legislature'.[13]

There is no uniform practice for the Governors to invite the leader of the single largest party to form the government. To quote Dr. Jennings, 'The Queen's task is only to secure a government, not to try to form a government which is likely to forward a policy which she approves'.[14] Thus the role of the Governor, in the appointment of the Chief Minister, is to be guided by the basic principles of parliamentary democracy rather than by his real discretion.

Dismissal of a Chief Minister

The Constitution of India under Article 164(1) lays down that the Ministers shall hold office during the pleasure of the Governor. At the same time the same Article under Clause (2) lays down that the Council of Ministers shall be collectively responsible to the Legislative Assembly. It means so long as the Council of Ministers enjoys the confidence of the Assembly, the Ministry continues to enjoy the pleasure of the Governor.

Theoretically the Governor may exercise "his discretionary power to dismiss a particular ministry. But this discretionary power is not generally exercised when there is a clear violation of any of the express provisions of the Constitution".[15] Otherwise the duty of the Governor is to advise the Ministry, to warn the Ministry, to suggest alternatives and ask for a reconsideration.[16] As a Parliamentary convention, the Ministry resigns when no confidence motion is passed against it. In spite of these conventions and decency, a defeated Ministry in a State may refuse to resign even after vote of no confidence against it. Here the Governor should exercise his discretion to dismiss the Ministry. If the Governor is satisfied that the Ministry no longer enjoys the majority support of the Assembly due to defections, split in the party, floor crossing, etc., he should ask the Chief Minister to prove his strength in the Assembly. If the Chief Minister is not able to face the Assembly and show his strength, the Governor may dismiss the Ministry and install another Ministry having working majority in the Assembly. For example in 1967, the Chief Minister of the first United Front Ministry Ajoy Kumar Mukherjee could not face the Assembly at different stages. As a result, the Governor, Dharma Vira withdrew his pleasure and dismissed the Ministry on November 21, 1967. A new Ministry headed by P.C. Gosh was installed in West Bengal on the same day.[17] Sometimes the Governor can exercise his discretion in lengthening or shortening the life span of the Ministry. In Uttar Pradesh, C.B. Gupta's Ministry was reduced into minority in November 1969 on account of split in the All India Congress. But the Ministry continued in February 10, 1970, the Governor of Punjab, Dr. D.C. Pavate did not make haste in recommending the President's rule in the State when the Badal Ministry was reduced to minority following the withdrawal of the coalition partner, Jana Sangh.[18]

In Assam also "On the 6th December, 1980, an eight-member Congress(I) Ministry headed by Mrs. Anwar Timur was sworn in at Janata Bhawan at Dispur"[19] by dismissing the Assam Janata Legislative Party by the Governor.

"Dalan Chandra Baruah, the Deputy Leader of the Assam Janata Party said that the installation of the Congress(I) Government in the State was unconstitutional and in clear violation of the existing laws and established democratic conventions...The Governor should have asked different political groups in the assembly to submit lists of their members. He should have then invited the leader of the single largest group...the Governor did not follow this practice and invited the Congress(I) enjoyed the support of only 55 MLAs".[20]

On May 11, 1984, the Governor of Sikkim, "J.R. Taleyarkhan announced that the Chief Minister Nar Bahadur Bhandari had been dismissed under Article 164(1) which reads that 'the Ministers shall hold office during the pleasure of the Governor'. He appointed Bhim Bahadur Gurung as the Chief Minister of the State in a four-men-Ministry of Congress(I).[21]

Similarly "in July 1984, Jammu and Kashmir Governor Jagmohan dismissed the National Conference Ministry led by Dr. Farooq Abdullah on the ground of defection without giving any chance to show majority strength in the Assembly and installed the Congress(I) Ministry of G.M. Shah the same evening".[22]

Again, in August 1984, the Governor of Andhra Pradesh, Ramlal refused to verify the supporters of the Chief Minister, N.R. Rama Rao and curtly said, 'No need I am satisfied that you have lost the majority'. He hurriedly took the oath taking ceremony of N. Bhaskar Rao [Congress(I)] as Chief Minister in the State.[23]

The ruling Congress led by Hokeshe Soma in Nagaland suffered a split when 13 MLAs broke away from the Congress and formed a new party and merged with the other opposition groups in August 1980. The Governor K.V. Krishna Rao refused to consider the formation of an alternative Government on the ground that the new grouping was (a) devoid of any ideology, (b) did not have any object of service, and (c) member of the group had connections with the Naga underground and recommended President's Rule and dissolution of the Assembly".[24]

In September 1988 also, in Meghalaya, "Governor Hiteshwar Saikia obviously took action under instruction from the Central Home Ministry, dismissed the Mizoram National Front Ministry of Laldenga. Thereafter, President Rule was proclaimed and the Assembly was simultaneously dissolved".[25]

After the National Front Government at the centre, in Nagaland the Congress(I) Government headed by S.C. Jamir became minority as 12 MLAs defected from the party and the Government M.M

Thomas, a Janata appointee dismissed the Jamir ministry and K.L. Chisi was invited to form the government and prove his majority in the House in 30 days".[26]

The above examples show that different Governors have acted differently in dismissing the Chief Minister or the Ministry. In short there is no uniform convention for the dismissal of the State Ministry by the Governor. The exercise of the discretionary power of the Governor very much depends upon the political situations and atmosphere prevailing in the State.

Summoning of the State Legislature

Under Article 171(1) of the Constitution of India, 'the Governor shall from time to time summon the House or each House of the Legislature of the State to meet at such time and place as he thinks fit, but six months shall not intervene between the last sitting and the next session'. Generally the Governor has to exercise this power according to the advice of the Chief Minister. But the Constitution empowers him to summon each house of the Legislature from time to time as he thinks fit. Here we can examine two points, i.e., (i) is the Governor entitled to convene the Assembly session without the advice of the Chief Minister? (ii) can the Governor convene the Assembly session contrary to the advice of the Chief Minister when there is doubt about majority support in the House? Two views may be examined. The first view is expressed by persons like K. Santhanam and others. According to them, the Governor is entitled to call session if he thinks that the Ministry is trying to evade its responsibilities under the Constitution.[27] The Governor can convene the sitting of the Assembly even with the absence of the Chief Minister's advice. The second view is held by persons like Dr. L.M. Singhvi. That is, when there is enough reason to belief that the Chief Minister and the Council of Ministers do not command the support of a clear majority in the Legislative Assembly, the Governor can, in his discretion take steps to ascertain the position".[28] In a situation of defection from the ruling party, the Governor has to watch the latest trends of the political development. If he thinks that the majority of the ruling party is in doubt because of the defection or the split in the party or in the United group, he should ask the Chief Minister to face the Assembly. Because under Article 159, the Governor has the constitutional duty to protect the law of the land.

Proroguing the Sitting of the Assembly

Article 174(2)(a) of the Constitution of India lays down that 'the Governor may from time to time prorogue the House or either House'. Proroguegation means bringing the session of the Assembly to an end until a fixed date.

As a parliamentary convention in India, the Governor exercises this function on the advice of the Council of Ministers. The question is whether the Governor always prorogues the Assembly only on the advice of the Council of Ministers or not? There are examples to show that on many political issues and constitutional crisis, the Governor prorogues the Assembly independently. For example, D.C. Pavate the Governor of Punjab prorogued the Legislative Assembly on April 10, 1970 while the resolution for the removal of the Speaker was there.[29]

Dissolution of the State Legislature

According to Article 174(2)(b), the Governor is entitled to exercise the power to dissolve the Legislative Assembly of the State. The Constitution of India does not provide any norm to regulate the power of dissolution of the Assembly except the single sentence, i.e., 'the Governor may from time to time dissolve the Legislative Assembly'.

In normal times, there are two ways for the dissolution of the State Assembly, i.e., (i) after the expiry of the term of five years, and (ii) under Article 174(2)(a), the Governor can dissolve the Assembly when he is satisfied that their is no party or coalition of parties to form a State government. The Governor usually dissolves the State Assembly on the advice of the Chief Minister. The question is whether the Governor is bound to accept the advice of the Chief Minister for the dissolution of the State Assembly. An analysis of the Article 174(2)(a) indicates that the Governor is not to be influenced by the Chief Minister in exercising his discretion to dissolve the Assembly when he has reason to believe that the constitutional machinery can be carried on in accordance with the provisions of the Constitution without dissolving the Assembly of the State.

There is no uniform convention regarding the exercise of discretionary power by the Governor. Different Governors exercise their discretion differently in granting or refusing the dissolution of the State Assembly.

Getting or Seeking Information from the Chief Minister on Both Legislative and Administrative Matters

According to Article 167(a), it is the duty of the Chief Minister to communicate to the Governor of the State all decisions of the Council of Ministers on all administrative and legislative affairs of the State. The Governor does not take part in meetings of the Council of Ministers. The Chief Minister has to communicate all decisions to the Governor. He has also to inform the Governor about the proposals for legislation from time to time. 'It shall be the duty of the Chief Minister of each State to furnish each information relating to the administration of the affairs of State and proposals for legislation from time to time. It shall be the duty of the Chief Minister of each State to furnish each information relating to the administration of the affairs of State and proposals for legislation as the Governor may call for.[30] It means that the Governor has the Constitutional right to ask the Chief Minister for any information relating it the affairs of State administration. In other words, the Governor may exercise his discretionary power in asking the Chief Minister for information relating to the affairs of the State.

Since the enforcement of the Constitution of India, there is no common practice among the Chief Ministers in providing or furnishing information to the Governors. Different Chief Ministers behave differently in dealing the Governors of there respective States. But the Governor has to see that the laws of the country is always protected. If not, the Governor, can ask the Chief Minister to provide any information relating to the affairs of the State.

To Give Assent to a Bill or Return the Bill

Article 200 of the Constitution of India gives discretionary power to the Governor in giving assent to a bill passed by the State legislature, the Governor may give his assent or may withhold his assent or may reserve the bill for the consideration of the President. In such matters he requires no advice from the Chief Minister or the Council of Ministers. He should decide the case on his own judgement. In withholding his assent to a bill, the Governor has to give reasons that the bill after becoming a law may affect the national security and fundamental interest of the State. The Constitution does not provide any time limit for withholding a bill by the Governor. The Governor may return a bill except money bill to the legislature for reconsideration or modification. The House or Houses will reconsider the bill accordingly, i.e., in the light of amendments or suggestion proposed by the Governor.

To Reserve a Bill for the Consideration of the President

The Governor may reserve a bill for the consideration of the President in the following matter:

(1) When a bill passed by the State Legislature affects the independence, dignity and status of the State judiciary; and

(2) When a bill is inconsistent with any provision of law enacted by Parliament or if it is contrary to the existing law of the country.

In addition to the above, there are certain provisions in the Constitution of India under which the Governor can exercise his discretion to reserve a bill for the assent of the President. (a) If the bills passed by the Assembly is related to taxation in respect of water or electricity, then under Article 288(1)(2), the Governor has to reserve the bill for assent of the President; (b) If the passed bill affects the operation of Article 360 of the Constitution of India, the Governor has to reserve the bill for the consideration of the President; (c) Under Article 304(b) of the Constitution of India, the Governor may reserve those bills which impose some restrictions on the freedom of trade and commerce; and (d) The Governor may also reserve those bills which he thinks to unconstitutional or contrary to the Directive Principles of State Policy.

Promulgation of Ordinance

One of the most important discretionary power of the Governor is the promulgation of ordinance. Under Article 213(3) (when the Legislature of the State is not in session), if the Governor is satisfied that circumstances has arisen which render it necessary for him to take immediate action, he may promulgate ordinances. The important question is whether the Governor exercises this power on the advice of the Council of Ministers or not? Theoretically this power belongs to the Governor. But practically, he exercises this power on the advice of Council of Ministers. Then a question arises whether this power can be described as a discretionary power of the Governor or not? There are two views. One view led by D.D. Basu says that it is not a discretionary power of the Governor. He must exercise this power with the advice of Ministers.[31] The second view was led by persons like D.C. Pavate, former Governor of Punjab that the Governor shall not always be guided by the Council of Ministers in issuing ordinances. He has to examine the basis, the purpose and objective of issuing ordinances. To quote him, 'I had taken an oath in the name of Government that I would to the best of my ability preserve, protect and defend the Constitution. If I had reason to think that there was no particular urgency or that it could lead to political corruption. I sent back the ordinance or talk the matter over with the Chief Minister and explain to him my difficulties in issuing the ordinance'.[32]

Under Article 213 of the Constitution of India, it the personal satisfaction and responsibility that an ordinance can be issued. "It is required to see that circumstance exist which render it necessary for you to take immediate action, and to promulgate such an ordinance".[33]

The Governor has to see that such ordinances are in accordance with healthy traditions where public interest is involved. Such discretion was applied by the Punjab Governor, Dr. D.C. Pavate when the Akali led coalition Ministry headed by P.S. Badal advised the Governor to issue an ordinance for the appointment of the legislators to be the member of the Board and corporation. The Governor asked the urgency of issuing such ordinance. Thus before issuing ordinances, the Governor must satisfy himself that there are circumstances which compels him to take an appropriate step for public interest. The Governor can also withdraw an ordinance. Before promulgation of an ordinance, the previous instruction of the President under the conditions laid down in (a), (b) and (c) of Article 213 of the Constitution of India is necessary.

Reporting to the President regarding the Breakdown of Constitutional machinery in the State:

Under Article 356 of the Constitution of India, the governor is the only authority in the State reporting the breakdown of Constitutional machinery in the State. Only on receipt of a report from the Governor, the President can proclaim a state of emergency and impose President's Rule in the State. From this Article, we know that the Governor has to act in his discretion in making report to the President. It is true that the Governor being a Constitutional head of the State has to act on the advice of the Council of Ministers. But he should apply his individual judgement whether he should accept the advice of the Council of Minister or not?

Even after a fresh election in a State, if no party secures majority the Governor has to exercise his discretion by reporting the matter to the President about the failure of Constitutional machinery in the State. Again if the Governor thinks that there is political instability in the State due to defection, he may exercise his discretionary power in recommending President's Rule in the

State. In 1971, Mysore and Gujarat had President's rule due to defections. In 1973, the ruling party in Orissa lost majority due to defections. The Governor did invite the leader of the second largest party to form the Ministry. In the same manner, the Governors of Nagaland and Goa in 1975 and in 1979 respectively exercised their discretionary power and recommended for President's Rule in the two States. Of course the recommendation of the Governor may not be accepted by the President. For instance in 1977 in spite of the recommendations from the Governors, President's rule was imposed in nine States of northern India by dissolving the Legislative Assemblies. It may be remembered that there was Janata rule at the centre and some State Ministries were Congress ruled, and other were headed by regional parties like Akali Dal in Punjab, D.M.K. in Tamil Nadu etc.[34] The nine States were Punjab, Haryana, Himachal Pradesh, Uttar Pradesh, Bihar, Madhya Pradesh, Rajasthan, Orissa and West Bengal.

Special Power under the Sixth Schedule of the Constitution of India

The Sixth Schedule of the Constitution of India contains provisions for the administration of tribal areas of Assam, Meghalaya, Tripura and Mizoram. Major portion of this Schedule is dealt with the discretionary power of the Governor though the word 'discretion' is not mentioned. Under clause 1(3) of the Schedule, the Governor has the power to include any area, to exclude any area, to create an autonomous district, to increase its area, to diminish the area, to unite any two or more autonomous districts. The Governor can also alter the name of any autonomous district and define its boundaries. The Governor has also the power to nominate four members of the District Council. He has also the power to make rule for the first Constitution of the District Council. Under clause 4(3) of the Schedule, the Governor has power to empower the High Court to exercise its jurisdiction oversuits and cases related to village councils from time to time. Under clause 5(1), the Governor has also the power to try offences punishable with death, transportation for life or imprisonment. Prior approval of the Governor is necessary for the establishment of primary schools, dispensaries, market roads, etc. Under clause 7(2) of the Schedule, the Governor has to make rules for the management of the District fund and Regional fund. The Governor has discretionary power to determine the amount payable by the State to the District Council under clause 9(2) of the Schedule. Under clause 14(1) of the Schedule, the Governor can appoint a commission to enquire into and report on the administration of autonomous districts and autonomous regions. The Governor has also the power of a District or a Regional Council and order a fresh election.

In exercising the above powers, the Governor is not to be guided by the advice of the Council of Ministers. There is nothing in the Schedule that he should accept the advice of the Council of Ministers.

Power under Article 371 of the Constitution of India

Article 371 of the Constitution of India gives a series of discretionary powers into hand of the Governor. For example, the Governor of Nagaland has special responsibility for the maintenance of law and order in the State. But he has to exercise this discretionary power after consulting the Council of Ministers. Regarding Tuenshang district, the Governor has certain special powers like administration, equitable allocation of money between Tuenshaing district and the rest of the State sanctioned by the Government of India. Without the permission of the Governor, the laws, acts passed by the legislature of Nagaland cannot be applied to Tuenshang district. The Governor in his discretion has power to make the final decision on all matters relating to Tuenshang district. The Governor in his discretion has the power to make the final decision on all matters relating to Tuenshang district.

MANIPUR

Like the Governors of other States, the Governor of Manipur also enjoys certain discretionary power since the inauguration of

Manipur as a fullfledged State in 1972. He was also the Governor of Assam, Meghalaya, Nagaland and Tripura. The discretionary power exercised by the Governor of Manipur may be examined under the following heads.

Appointment of the Chief Minister

After the election of March 1972, the Ministry in Manipur was formed by the United Legislature Party consisting of 15 MPP, 3 SSP, 1 Congress(O) and 13 Independents. In the appointment of the Chief Minister of this MPP led ULP coalition Government, the Governor B.K. Nehru, had no alternative but to appoint the leader of the MPP, Md. Alimuddin as Chief Minister because he was unanimously elected as the leader of the coalition. On the other hand, the Governor did not invite the leader of the progressive Democratic Alliance to form the Ministry in March 1973 though the Alliance claimed the support of 32 MLAs. The same happened after the mid-term election of 1974. The united legislature party consisting of MPP, SSP, MHU and Independents elected Md. Alimuddin as the leader unanimously. Accordingly the Governor appointed Md. Alimuddin as the Chief Minister ignoring the claim of the leader of the Congress Party. After about three months, i.e., in July 1974, the Governor had to appoint Yangmaso Shaiza as the Chief Minister of the progressive Democratic Front Ministry consisting of Congress(R), ULP, MHU and Manipur Democratic party. Soon a rift cropped up between the Government and the Congress party. As a result a section of the Congress withdrew its support. A Democratic Legislature Party was formed comprising the Congress and the ULP.[35] Political mongering was continued at a high pitch and separate camps were established in order to confine the MLAs in the camps. The leader of the Democratic Legislature party, R.K. Dorendro Singh claimed that he enjoyed the majority support and requested the Governor to invite him to form the ministry. Before exercising his discretionary power the Governor called and heard the 3 MLAs who were in the camp of Shaiza. The three MLAs expressed their support for the Congress. ULP coalition. The Governor exercised his discretionary power by inviting R.K. Dorendro Singh to form the Government.

After the Lok Sabha election of March 1977, there was large scale defection in Manipur. As a result the Congress party was reduced to a minority. By the end of June 1977, the strength of the Janata party had increased to more than 50 in a House of 60 members. The Governor had no alternative but to invite the leader of the Janata party, Yangmaso Shaiza to form the ministry. In the Assembly election of January 1980, no party secured majority in the Legislature Assembly of Manipur. The Congress party was able to collect MLAs belonging to Congress(O), MPP, KNA and Independents in order to form a coalition ministry. It was not difficult for the Governor L.P. Singh to invite the leader of the Congress(I), R.K. Dorendro Singh to form the ministry.

On March 1988, Manipur witnessed a political scene where the Governor, General K.V. Krishna Rao had to appoint R.K. Jaichandra Singh as the Chief Minister of the State. It was due to the dissident politics within the Congress Legislature Party. Here the action of the Governor was more guided by the decision of the Central Government and Congress High Command than anything else. The new Chief Minister had to face a bye election in order to legalise his position.

In the Assembly election of February 1990, no party secure majority. The Congress party emerged as the largest single party securing 26 seats. On the other hand, United Front was formed by opposition parties like Janata Dal, MPP, Congress(S), CPI, KNA, CPI(M), and NPP. The Front claimed that it had the support of 32 MLAs.[36] The leader of the Congress(I) party, R.K. Dorendro Singh also requested the Governor, to invite him to form the Government. The Governor, Chintamani Panigrahi, after observing the political situation exercised his discretionary power by inviting the leader of the United Front, R.K. Ranabir Singh to form the Government.[37] It may be noted that the National Front Ministry at the Centre partly influenced the Governor in taking his decision.

Dismissal of Chief Minister or Ministry

It is the common practice of the Governor to dismiss a Chief Minister or Ministry when it loses the majority support of the Assembly. In Manipur the first MPP led ULP coalition ministry led by Md. Alimuddin lost majority support on March 1973. The Progressive Democratic Alliance formed by the Congress, CPI and PIG had the strength of as many as 32 MLAs. The Chief Minister failed to prove the majority support in the session of the Assembly. The Governor B.K. Nehru carefully observed the political atmosphere and development prevailing in the State. Before taking his action to dismiss the Ministry, the Chief Minister submitted his resignation. The same happened in 1974 when the second MPP led coalition ministry lost the majority support. The Progressive Democratic front Ministry of July 1974 led by Yangmaso Shaiza and the Congress nominees in the ministry. Yangmaso Shaiza refused to accept the nominees of the Congressmen.[38] The ULP also withdrew its support. The Shaiza Ministry was reduced to minority and the Governor was about to dismiss the ministry. But the ministry resigned on 5 December, 1974 and the Congress-CPI coalition ministry of July 1975 led by R.K. Dorendro Singh was reduced to a minority due to defections. The Governor L.P. Singh did not exercise his discretionary power to dismiss the ministry as the Chief Minister tendered his resignation.

Manipur had witnessed the first example of the dismissal of ministry on November 1979. The Janata party suffered a setback when 9 MLAs led by R.K. Dorendro Singh, former Chief Minister of Manipur resigned from the Party on 6 October, 1978 and decided to join Congress(I).[39] The CPI demanded immediate resignation of the Janata Ministry. It denounced the steps taken by the Shaiza ministry and strongly condemned the declaration of the whole of Manipur valley as a disturbed area and the use of the most hated Armed Forces (Assam and Manipur) Special Power Act 1958.[40] The Congress party also launched Satyagraha Movement since 11 September, 1978 demanding the dissolution of the Ministry headed by Y. Shaiza; N. Tomi Congress MP from Manipur and 10 other

MPS have demanded the dissolution of the Assembly and Ministry. Opposition member belonging to the Congress(I) and the CPI boycoted the Governor's address on the opening day of the budget session of the Assembly as a protest against the failure of the Government to maintain law and order and to fulfil the minimum aspirations of the masses.[41] In the meantime the activities of the extremists increased killing many government officials. Eight political parties of Manipur, i.e., the Congress, the Congress(I), the CPI(M), the Lok Dal, the Manipur Peoples' Party, the Ereibak Leishem Party and the Kuki National Assembly unanimously resolved to request the President, N. Sanjiva Reddy and the Central leaders to dissolve the outlined Manipur legislative Assembly and the dismissal of the Janata ministry.[42] All these developments called for the exercise of discretionary power of the Governor I.P. Singh for dismissal of the Janata ministry. Accordingly the ministry was dissolved by a Presidential order issued under Article 356 of the Constitution on 14th November, 1979. The Governor in his report has drawn attention to the deteriorating law and order situation in Manipur and said that 'the administration had been rendered increasingly ineffective in dealing with the activities of extremists because of gross maladministration, favouritism and nepotism.[43] The Chief Minister of Congress(I) led coalition Ministry of January 1980, R.K. Dorendro Singh also faced a political crisis caused mainly by defection of 11 members to the opposition. Because of this, the Governor L.P. Singh had to exercise his discretionary power of dismissing the Chief Minister and his ministry. In 1986, there were many allegations against the Chief Minister Rishang Keishing that he was involved in corruption activities. The allegation was raised mainly by I. Tompok, Education Minister; L. Lalit, Finance Minister; and Saso Lorho, Agriculture Minister. Dissident politics was very active during the period. The Governor Gen. K.V. Krishna Rao, did not use his discretion. Rather he consulted the Centre and waited for advice. Rishang Keishing, in spite of many charges of corruption, bribery and maladministration enjoyed absolute majority in the Assembly. But at the late night of the 4th March, 1988, the Governor on the advice of the Central

Government dismissed Rishang Keishing from the Chief Ministership on the ground that he supported insurgency in Manipur.[44]

Summoning of the State Legislature

Like the Governor of other Indian States, the Governor of Manipur summons the session of the Legislative Assembly from time to time. Generally the Governor exercises his power according to the advice of the Chief Minister. At the first session of every year, the Governor gave an address in which has gives an outline of the policy and programme of the Government.

Proroguing the Sitting of the Assembly

Generally the Governor prorogues the State Assembly on the advice of the Chief Minister. The session of the State Assembly usually came to an end when the Governor prorogues the Assembly until a fixed date. In Manipur, there was no political issues and constitutional crisis where the Governors exercised their discretionary power by getting contrary to the advice rendered by the Chief Minister. There were only the causes of adjournment of the Assembly *sine die* when the Ministry faced political crisis. For example, on March 1973, the Assembly was adjourned *sine die* by the Speaker when the first MPP led coalition ministry faced a vote of no confidence. In 1974 also, the session of the Assembly was adjourned *sine die* when four ministers of the second MPP led ULP Ministry resigned from ULP Ministry and joined PDF.

Dissolution of the State Assembly

The Governor of Manipur dissolves the Legislative Assembly of Manipur after the expiry of the term of five years. But there were causes of dissolution of the State Assembly before the completion of the term of five years. First in 1973, the Governor, L.P. Singh used his discretionary power and recommended for the dissolution of the Assembly when he was satisfied that there was no party or coalition of parties to form a stable government. It may be remembered that the Congress led Progressive Democratic Alliance, having the support of 32 members requested the Governor to allow them to form the Government.[45] The next was in 1979 when the Janata Ministry (1977-1979) led by Yangmaso Shaiza faced charges of corruption, maladministration and nepotism. The charges were levelled mainly by opposition parties like the Congress(I), the CPI, the CPI(M), the Lok Dal, the Manipur Peoples' Party, the Ereibak Leishem Party, the Kuki National Assembly, etc. The Governor L.P. Singh recommended to the Centre for the dissolution of the Assembly and Ministry. Here the political atmosphere and circumstances forced the Governor to exercise his discretionary power to dissolve the Assembly. Here the Governor did not accept the advice of the Chief Minister. Other cases of dissolution were normal dissolution, i.e., after the end of the five year term of the Assembly. The Governor usually allowed the outgoing Ministry in power to remain as a caretaker government till the fresh General Election. For example in 1984, the Governor allowed Rishang Keishing Ministry (Congress) to remain as a caretaker Ministry after the dissolution of the Assembly. In February 1990, the Congress(I) Ministry led by R.K. Jaichandra Singh remained as a caretaker government after the dissolution of the Assembly.

Getting or Seeking Information from the Chief Minister

The Chief Minister of Manipur, starting from 1972 onwards, duly informed the Governor of what happened in the Ministry, in the government and in the State. It was after getting relevant information from the Chief Ministers and the Governor sometimes exercised discretionary power. During the period of political instability in Manipur, i.e., from 1972 to 1977, the Governor was very cautious in exercising his powers relating to the formation and expansion of Ministry. In May 1977, the Chief Minister R.K. Dorendro Singh supplied to the Governor all the relevant informations for forming a pure Congress Ministry. The Governor

L.P. Singh after getting information from the Chief Minister and after observing the political situation allowed him to do so.[46] Sometimes the Governor acted contrary to the information or advice tendered by the Chief Minister. For example in 1977, the Governor L.P. Singh did not listen Chief Minister Yangmaso Shaiza's plea that the Government was functioning smoothly and the law and order situation was under control. The Governor recommended for President's Rule in the State. In the report, the Governor recommended for President's Rule in the State. In the report, the Governor has drawn attention to the deteriorating law and order situation in Manipur and said, 'the administration had been rendered increasingly ineffective in dealing with the activities of extremists because of gross maladministration, favouritism and nepotism.[47] Another instance was in 1985, the Chief Minister Rishang Keishing met the Governor Gen. K.V. Krishna Rao regarding the expansion of his ministry. But the Governor did not allow the Chief Minister to expand the Ministry before solving the internal crisis of the Congress Legislature Party.[48] Without informing the Governor, the Chief Minister cannot do anything regarding the appointment and dismissal of Ministers. In August 1986, the Chief Minister Rishang Keishing tried to dismiss the three Cabinet Ministers namely L. Lalit Singh, I. Tompok Singh and Soso Lorho in the absence of the Governor General K.V. Krishna Rao.[49] But it was not effective. As a matter of fact, this sort of indifferent attitude of the Chief Minister is really undemocratic. It is the constitutional duties of the Chief Minister to inform the Governor about the changes, developments and happenings in the State. The Governor is not merely the constitutional head of the State but also a functionary to discharge certain duties through the constitutional device.

To give Assent to Bill or Return the Bill

Generally all bills passed the Manipur Legislative Assembly become a law or an Act after getting the assent from the Governor. The Governor may give his assent to a bill, he may withhold his assent therefrom or he may reserve the bill for the consideration of the President. The Governor of Manipur gave his assent to most of the bills passed by the Manipur Legislative Assembly. Sometimes the Governor returned a bill for the reconsideration of the Assembly. For example, the Manipur Rifles Police Force Bill 1984 had been sent to the Governor for his assent. The Governor S.M. Burney returned the Bill to the Assembly after making some observations. 'I return the bill with a request for reconsideration in respect of clause 5(2) for such amendment as the House may consider proper. It appears to me the clause 5(2) has been put in the negative form and of happily worded'.[50]

To Reserve a Bill for the Consideration of the President

The Governor of Manipur reserve some bills passed by the Manipur Legislative Assembly for the consideration of the President. In March 1978, the Manipur Legislative Assembly unanimously passed the Manipur Official Language Bill 1978 designating Manipuri 'written in Bengali script' as the official language of the State. The hill peoples are afraid that if the Manipuri language, i.e., the language of the Meiteis is the official language of the State, they would be at a disadvantage.[51] It might be possible of this that the Governor L.P. Singh reserved the Bill for the consideration of the President. Thus the Governor exercised his discretionary power to reserve a bill for the consideration of the President in the interest of the people and the State.

Governor's Power to Promulgate Ordinance

The Governor of Manipur promulgate ordinance when the Legislative Assembly was not in session. In most cases, these ordinances were issued on the advice of the Council of Ministers. In 1975 during the Chief Ministership of R.K. Dorendro Singh, the Governor L.P. Singh promulgated two ordinances namely the Manipur Legislature (Removal or Disqualification) (Amendment) Ordinance 1975 and the Manipur Land Revenue and Land Reforms Ordinance 1975 on 20th January, 1975.[52] In the same year, the Chief

Minister R.K. Dorendro Singh advised the Governor L.P. Singh to issue two ordinances namely the Manipur Local Funds (Account and Audit) Ordinance 1975 and the Manipur Agricultural Indebtedness Relief Ordinance 1975. In 1976, five ordinances namely, (1) the Departmentalisation of Union Accounts (Transfer or Personal 1976, (2) the Manipur Co-operative Societies Ordinance 1976, (3) the Manipur Land Revenue and Land Reforms (Validation of Proceedings) Ordinances 1976, and (4) the Manipur Agricultural Credit Operation and Miscellaneous Provision (Banks) Ordinance 1976, and (5) the Metal Corporation (Nationalisation and Miscellaneous Provisions) Ordinance 1976 were promulgated by the Governor on the advice of the Council of Ministers headed by R.K. Dorendro Singh. In 1977, three ordinances were issued by the Governor L.P. Singh, two of them, the Police (Manipur Third Amendment) Ordinance 1977 and the Metal Corporation (Nationalisation and Miscellaneous Provisions) Ordinance 1977 during the Janata rule, the Chief Minister being Yangmaso Shaiza. On the advice of the Council of Ministers headed by Yangmaso Shaiza, the Governor L.P. Singh promulgated three ordinances in 1978 namely the Manipur Municipalities (Second Amendment) Ordinance 1978, the Manipur Public Premises (Eviction of Unauthorized Occupants) Ordinance 1978 and the Manipur Parliamentary Secretary (Salary and Allowances) Ordinance 1978 and two in 1979, i.e., the Manipur Highways Ordinance 1979 and the Manipur Panchayati Raj (Second Amendment) Ordinance 1979.[53]

Reporting to the President regarding the Breakdown of Constitutional Machinery in the State

In exercising the discretionary power of reporting to the President regarding the breakdown of constitutional machinery in the State' the Governor is not always bound by the advice of the Chief Minister or of the Council of Ministers. In Manipur this power was first exercised by the Administrator in October 1967, i.e., before the getting of statehood. The prevailing political situation and circumstances rather forced the Administrator to exercise this power. The membership of the opposition party, i.e., the Congress and the ruling party, United Front were equally balanced, i.e., 16/16 on each side when the no confidence motion was discussed on 24 October 1967. The Chief Commissioner of Manipur exercised this power in October, 1969 again when the 'no-confidence motion' against the Ministry was supported by 19 members against 12. The Chief Commissioner reported to the President that there is the breakdown of constitutional machinery in the State so President's Rule was imposed. The Chief Commissioner, Baleswar Prasad accepted the advice of the Chief Minister in recommending President's Rule in the State. The next was in 1973, when the Governor B.K. Nehru recommended for the dissolution of the Assembly and imposition of President's Rule in the State. The Governor did not accept the request of the Congress led progressive Democratic Alliance to form the Government. Here the Governor was guided by the real political situation and crisis in the State. It may be noted that the Congress was the ruling party at the Centre. In 1977, with the formation of Janata Government at the Centre, there were defections of 25 members from Congress to Janata Party. The Congress government led by R.K. Dorendro Singh was reduced to a minority. The Governor L.P. Singh after observing the prevailing political trend in the State reported to the Centre for the suspension of the Legislative Assembly and imposition of President's Rule. His recommendation was accepted by the President and thereby President's Rule was imposed in the State on 16 May, 1977. The next was in 1979 when there was strong allegation and charges against the Janata Ministry hosted by Yangmaso Shaiza. All opposition parties, i.e., the Congress, the CPI, etc., demanded the dissolution of the Assembly and dismissal of the Janata ministry. The allegations were the imposition of Armed Forces (Assam and Manipur) Special Power Act 1958, corruption of the Ministry at the highest level, failure of the government in maintaining the law and order and fulfilling minimum aspirations of the masses.[54] Another allegations was that the State Government was trying to delay the holding of elections to the State Assembly the term of which ended on 5 March, 1979.

But according to Chief Minister, Shaiza, there was no constitutional or organizational crisis in the State. The government was functioning smoothly and the law and order situation was under control. The Governor did not accept the view of the Chief Minister, Yangmaso Shaiza. He had exercised his discretionary power by reporting to the President that there is the breakdown of constitutional machinery in the State. In this report the Governor has drawn attention to the deteriorating law and order situation in Manipur and said that the administration had been rendered increasingly ineffective in dealing with the activities of extremists because of gross maladministration, favouritism and nepotism. In February 1981, the Governor L.P. Singh had to exercise his discretionary power of reporting and recommending for the imposition of President's Rule in the State. Due to defection of 11 members to the opposition, The Congress(I) led coalition ministry headed by R.K. Dorendro Singh falls on 27 February, 1981. The Governor after full observation of the political situation exercised this discriminatory power. In February 1990, the Governor's recommendation for the imposition of President's Rule was not accepted by the President for the first time in the political history of Manipur. Instead, the President allowed the Congress(I) Chief Minister R.K. Jaichandra Singh to remain as Caretaker Government.[55] The Governor, Chintamani Panigrahi in his report mentioned the deteriorating law and order situation in Manipur, the increase of anti-social and extremist activities, etc., in the State as basic reasons for the recommendation of President's Rule in the State.[56] It goes to the credit of the newly formed National Front Government at the Centre for allowing the Congress(I) Government to remain as Caretaker Government.[57]

Special Power of the Governor relating to the Bill Areas of Manipur

Manipur is not under the Sixth Schedule of the Constitution of India. So the Governor of Manipur does not have any special power under the Sixth Schedule. But he has some special power regarding the hill areas of Manipur. Article 371(c) provides certain discretionary power and responsibility into the hands of the Governor of Manipur. The Governor has the responsibility to constitute a committee, called Hill Areas Committee, of the Legislative Assembly of the State from the elected members of the Assembly from the hill areas of Manipur. The Governor has to guide the Hill Areas Committee for its proper functioning. If the Legislative Assembly passed any bill with amendments, modifications, change, etc., from the original one and submitted by the Hill Areas Committee, the Governor may send down the hill for reconsideration to the Legislative Assembly. In doing this, the Governor has to take into account the welfare of the hill people. Under clause 2 of the Article, the Governor had to send annual report to the President if required regarding the administration of the hill areas of Manipur.

Thus the Governor of Manipur is the pivot around which the politics of the State revolves. It is specially so when the Governor has to exercise his discretionary power very frequently in the 1970s and early 1980s. The stability and instability of Ministry and political system at large is depended upon the nature of exercising discretionary power of the Governor of Manipur. The Governor is quite impartial in exercising his discretionary power.

References

1. Banerjee, A.C. (ed), *Indian Constitutional Documents,* Vol. III, 2nd Edition, A. Mukherjee & Private Co., Calcutta, 1948, p. 281.
2. Rao, Shiva B.(ed), *The Framing of the Indian Constitution,* Vol. II, The Indian Institute of Public Administration, New Delhi, 1967, pp. 658-659.
3. Gehlot, N.S., *The Office of the Governor, Its Constitutional Image and Reality,* Chugh Publications, Allahabad, 1977, pp. 52-53.
4. Constituent Assembly Debate, Vol. VIII, p. 491.
5. *Ibid.*, p. 492.
6. *Ibid.*, p. 500.
7. Constituent Assembly Debates, Vol. X, p. 114.

8. Iqbal Narain 'The Governor, The Problem of Role Identification', *Journal of African and Asian Studies,* Vol. I, No. 2, Delhi, 1968, p. 175.
9. Gehlot, N.S., *op. cit.,* p. 67.
10. *The Statesman,* (Delhi), 14.3.1967.
11. *Ibid.,* 16.3.1971.
12. *Ibid.,* 25.3.1971.
13. *The Report of the Committee of Governors,* New Delhi, President's Secretariat, 1971, p. 29.
14. Sir Jennings, Ivor, *The British Constitution,* Cambridge University Press, Cambridge, 1968, 5th edn., p. 32.
15. Sarkar, R.C.S., 'The Office of the Governor, *The Journal of Constitution and a Parliamentary Studies,* Vol. 3, No. 1, New Delhi, 1969, p. 28.
16. Constituent Assembly Debates, Vol. 8, p. 546.
17. Gehlot, *op. cit.,* p. 89.
18. Gehlot, *op. cit.,* p. 90.
19. *Times of India,* 8.12.1980.
20. *Ibid.,* 15.12.1980.
21. Sunanda K. Datta Ray, *Himalayan Caprice*, "The Governor, Sage or Saboteur", pp. 158-159.
22. Upendra P., *A. Breach of Democracy, Ibid.*, p. 116.
23. Upendra P., *A Breach of Democracy, Ibid.*, p. 116.
24. Madhu Limaye, 'The Anti Defection Law', *The Telegraph,* 28.8.1990.
25. *Ibid.*
26. *Ibid.*
27. *The Statesman,* New Delhi, 11.11.1967.
28. *Ibid.*
29. *The Hindusthan Times,* New Delhi, 12.4.1970.
30. Article 167 (b). The Constitution of India.
31. Basu, D.D., *Commentary on the Constitution of India,* S.C. Sarkar & Sons (P) Ltd., Calcutta, 1954, p. 339.
32. Pavate, D.C., *My Days as Governor*, Vikas Publishing.
33. *Ibid.,* p. 152.
34. The *Simanta Patrika,* 19.2.1980.
35. *Simanta Patrika,* 2.12.1974.
36. Prajatantra, 22.2.1990.
37. Khollao, 22.2.1990, Huyen Lampao, 24.2.1990.
38. Th. Gokul Singh, *Defection in Manipur,* 1963-1977, Imphal, 1978, p. 13.
39. *Amrita Bazar Patrika,* 7.10.1978.
40. *Ibid.,* 30.7.1978.
41. *Ibid.,* 20.3.1979.

42. *Ibid.*, 15.11.1979.
43. *Ibid.*, 15.11.1979.
44. *Prajatantra*, 8.3.1988.
45. Ksh. Bimola Devi, *Government and Politics in Manipur*, Ph.D. thesis submitted to Gauhati University (unpublished), 1981, p. 164.
46. Ksh. Bimola Devi, *op. cit.*, p. 171.
47. *Amrita Bazar Patrika*, 15 November, 1979.
48. *Prajatantra*, 16 July, 1985.
49. *Huyen Lanpao*, 19 September, 1986.
50. Proceedings of the Fourth Manipur State Legislative Assembly, February 25, 1985, Vol. 4, p. 20.
51. Ken. Bimola Devi, *op. cit.*, p. 311.
52. Government of Manipur, Law Department, Ordinance, 1984.
53. *Ibid.*
54. *Amrita Bazar Patrika*, 20.3.1979.
55. *Huiyen Lalpao* 19.2.1990.
56. Khollao, 18.2.1990

Chapter-VI

The Governor and Centre-State Relations

The institution of the Governor is the most important organ through which the Union Government can maintain a liaison with the state governments in a federal state like India. During the British Rule there was a link between the Centre and the provinces through the Governor. The Governor General was in the Central level while the Governor of Bombay, Madras, etc., worked under the supervision of the Governor General.

The Constitution of India also provides a close relationship between the Union and the State through the institution of the Governor. The Governor is the constitutional as well as the administrative head of the State through which the Central Government can ensure whether the State Government acts in consistent with the policies and programmes of administration as set for by the Union Government.

The relation between the Governor as head of the State and the Union Government may be examined under the following heads:

(1) Appointment of the Governor;
(2) Removal of the Governor;
(3) Discretionary power of the Governor under Article 163 of the Constitution of India;
(4) Governor's power to reserve a bill passed by the State Legislature for the consideration of the President;

(5) Presidential sanction over certain ordinances;
(6) Union control over the State administration; and
(7) The Governor and the failure of the Constitutional machinery of the State.

1. The Different Heads are Discussed Below

Appointment of the Governor: Under Article 155 of the Constitution of India the Governor of the State is appointed by the President by warrant under his hand and seal. As he is appointed by the President he serves as a link between the Union Government and the Government of the State. In a word the Governor may be described as a Central nominee appointed by the President as head of the State. Thus under this Article 155, The Governor becomes the real handwork of the Central Government. Because in the Indian Parliamentary Democracy it is through the President that the Prime Minister appoints the State Governors. The President through his power of appointment can easily control the State Governors. That is why the Governor is said to be more an agent of the Union Government than the head of the State.

The Prime Minister and the Home Minister play a very important role in the appointment of the State Governor. The reality is that a Governor is dependent on the Prime Minister and the Home Minister for his appointment and removal. "As such as the Governor out of fear of losing his office or of not getting another international assignment on the expiry of his current term may need the prompting of the Union more carefully than the advice of his own Council of Ministers".[1] Practically, the President's task in the appointment of the Governor is a mere formality. It was the complaint of Dr. Rajendra Prasad, the first President of India that "he often read the appointment of Governors in the press and was officially approved only afterwards".[2]

There are criticisms regarding the appointment of the Governors by the President. One Lok Sabha member called Nath Pai "accused the Central Government of using the Governorship as a gift to the discredited, defeated and discarded politicians from the party and making mockery of the Constitution".[3] The statement was made in the Lok Sabha criticising the Centre for using the institution of the Governor as an instrument of the ruling party at the Centre. Because the ruling party in many cases appointed the Governors from its party pocket without concerning the concerned Chief Ministers. In the Constituent Assembly also some members "like Shri Brajeshwar Prasad opined that the President should be free from the influence of the Provincial Legislatures. The choice of the President should be unrestricted and unfettered while selecting the Governors for any province of the Union".[4] That was the main reason why majority of the members of the Constituent Assembly preferred the centrally appointed Governor. Regarding the establishment of a convention to concern the State Government, Alladi Krishnaswami Ayyar observed, "in normal working of the Constitution I have no doubt that the convention will grow up of the Government of India consulting the provincial Cabinet, in the selection of the Governor…"[5] However, K.T. Shah expressed the doubt whether such a convention of consulting the State Government prior to the selection of the Governor could grow up in India".[6] What K.T. Shah said is true regarding the appointment of the Governor still now. In the 1950s most of the Governors were appointed from the Congress party as there was the same party at both the Centre and States. There was no uniform policy for the Central Government in appointing the Governors. But after the General Elections of 1967 there were changes in the political scenario of the country. As a result of the change, the appointment of the Governor became a cause of tension between the Union and the States. The non-Congress Government of the States wanted the convention of consulting the ministry to be strictly observed. They favoured "not merely the consultation but the consent of the State Ministry concerned".[7] For example, in 1967, "the First United Front Government of West Bengal suggested the names of G.S. Pathak, a former Law Minister and Nityananda Kanungo, the then Governor of Gujarat to be appointed as the Governor of Bengal after the retirement of Miss Padma Naidu".[8] In spite of the suggestion made by the State Government, the Central government appointed Dharma Vira, the then Governor of Punjab and Haryana as the Governor of Bengal. Jyoti Basu, the then Deputy Minister of West Bengal was reported to have alleged that "the Centre had not consulted the State Chief Minister before appointing Dharma Vira as the Governor".[9] Likewise B.N. Chakravarti in Haryana and Nityanand Kanungo in Bihar were appointed Governor much against the wishes of the State Governments. In U.P. also C.P.N. Singh was appointed as Governor even without seeking the formal consent of the Lok Dal government.[10] This has created much friction between the Centre and the States. Sometimes this friction has resulted in the resignation of the Governor as it happened in West Bengal in 1960.

Sometimes the change in the ruling party in the Centre also resulted in the appointment of new Governors. In 1980, the newly formed Congress government under the Prime Ministership of Indira Gandhi appointed new Governors replacing the Governors appointed by the Janata Government. In 1990 also, the National Front Government under the Prime Ministership of V.P. Singh advised the President to appoint new Governors replacing those appointed during the Congress(I) regime. Accordingly the President R. Venkataraman appointed 16 new Governors—nine of the active politicians and the rest leading retired personalities.[11]

Thus the appointment of the Governors so far made are real and free choice of the ruling party at the Centre through the Indian President. Various suggestions are made in order to free the appointment of Governors from party politics. According to the Rajamannar Committee of Tamil Nadu, 'the Governor should be appointed always in consultation with the State Cabinet'. The Sarkaria Commission suggested that the concerned person should be consulted about the appointment. The Prime Minister should consult confidentially and informally the Vice President and the Speaker of the Lok Sabha. There must be effective consultation with the State Chief Minister in the selection of the Governor and the procedure of consultation should be prescribed in the Constitution itself. The Commission wants a suitable amendment to be incorporated in Article 155 which merely says that 'the

Governor of a State shall be appointed by the President by warrant under his hand and seal'.[12]

Removal of the Governor

Under Article 156 of the Constitution 'the Governor shall hold office during the pleasure of the President. This Article indicates that the Central Government absolutely enjoys the power for the removal of any State Governor at any time even without giving any reason. In other federal States of the world, the Constitution does not provide any provision for the removal of the State Governors. In USA, the State Governor is to be removed by the process of impeachment by the State legislative body. In Australia, the Governor holds office during the pleasure of the Governor General but he is not to be removed by the Govenor General at his discretion.

Many views have been expressed in the Constituent Assembly regarding the removal of the Governors. Prof. S.L. Saxena expressed, "if the Governor holds office during the pleasure of the President, it would completely take away the independence of the Governor. It only means that he must took to the President for continuing in office and so continue to be subservient to him."[13]

The Governors in the States were very easily removed before the expiry of his term by the President. For instance, the Governor of Tamil Nadu, Probhudas Patwari, a close friend of Morarji Dasai was removed on 26th October, 1980 when Indira Gandhi was Prime Minister of India. Similarly on 8th August, 1981, Raghukul Tilak, the Governor of Rajasthan was removed and no reason for his removal was given.[14] T.N. Singh, the Governor of West Bengal was also forced to resign as he refused to carry out blindly the directions given to him by the Centre.[15] The ruling party alleged that T.N. Singh had been removed from the Governorship of West Bengal with an ulterior motive of toppling the Left Front Government.

After the formation of National Front Government at the Centre headed by Prime Minister V.P. Singh, some of the State Governors have been asked by the President to tender their resignation so as to enable the Central Government to replace them. According to the Home Minister Mufti Mohammed Syed: "these Governors were not in tune with the changed political scenario following the Congress(I) defect in the last Lok Sabha election of November 1989".[16] In response to the desire of the President, the Governors of Haryana, Karnataka, Nagaland, Andhra Pradesh namely H.A. Brau, P. Venkata Subhaih, Dr. Gopal Singh and Mrs. Kumudben Joshi respectively quit the office of Governorship. Later on as many as ten Governors including the Governors of West Bengal, Tamil Nadu, Kerala, Goa, Himachal Pradesh, U.P., Orissa, Sikkim, Rajasthan and Arunachal Pradesh quit their office in accordance with the direction of the President.

From the above we know that the ruling political party at the Centre wants the same partymen to be the Governor of the States. That is why the Janata party while in power tried to remove many Governors appointed during the Congress regime. The Congress party also remove those Governors appointed during the Janata rule. According to H.R. Khanna, a former judge of the Supreme Court of India "Attempts to remove Governors of States with every change of Government at centre would give a partisan complexion to the office and project Governors as part of the political set-up at the centre. This would detract from a man's efficacy as a Governor, undermine confidence in his impartiality and make him suspect in the eyes of the other section of those in the State's political life".[17]

Another Supreme Court Judge V.R. Krishna Iyer has also decreed the practice of changing Governors with the change of Government at the Centre and described it as 'experiment in political pollution and trafficking in Governorships'.[18]

Discretion of the Governor under Article 163 of the Constitution

Article 163(1) of the Constitution of India mentions the existence of a council of Ministers to aid and advise the Governor. In spite of the provision, the same Article in 163(2) provides, 'if any question arise whether any matter is or is not a matter which the Governor is or under this Constitution required to act in his decision of the Governor in his discretion shall be final and the validity of anything done by the Governor shall not be called in question on the ground that he ought or ought not to have acted in his discretion. Thus the same article in the second part gives more emphasis to the discretion of the Governor rather than the binding of the council of Ministers. By the possession of this discretionary power, the Governor can easily act as an agent of the Centre by neglecting his Council of Ministers.

The post 1967 political history of India disturbed the political hegemony of one party rule in both the Centre and the States. The Governors exercised their discretionary powers under different pressing situation of the country. There are three grounds for exercising discretionary power by the Governor in order to maintain a close relationship with the Centre. They are (a) the appointment of the Chief Minister; (b) the dismissal of the Minister; and (c) the prorogation and dissolution of the Legislative Assembly.

Theoretically the Governor has to appoint the leader of the majority party in the Legislative Assembly as Chief Minister of the State. But in the selection and appointment of the Chief Minister, the Governor is very much influenced by the Central High Command or Central Government. In such cases, the Governor is bound to appoint the Chief Minister as directed by the central Government. For example, in 1982, Prakash Malhotra, the Governor of Assam appointed K.C. Gogoi as the Chief Minister of the State in spite of the claim of S.C. Sinha who submitted a list of 65 supporters. 'Gogoi had only a strength of 13 supporters. The Governor did so to have Congress(I) Government in Assam to resolve the foreign nationals tangle'.[19]

The Central Government can help the State Government in resolving a problem or a crisis in the State if the ruling party at both the Centre and the State is the same. The political understanding and adjustment is usually done through the Governor.

In the dismissal of a ministry in the State, the action of the Governor is very often influenced by the politics of the Central

Government. One can find such an example in Nagaland in 1988. After the defection of 13 MLAs from the Hokesi Sema's Congress(I) Ministry in July 1988, the opposition formed the Nagaland Peoples' Council under the leadership of Vamuzo. The Peoples' party had the support of 35 members in a House of 60. The leaders requested the Governor K.V. Krishna Rao to allow them to form the Government. But on the recommendation of the Governor, the President R. Venkataraman issued an order for the imposition of President's Rule in the State.[20]

Regarding the prorogation and dissolution of the Legislative Assembly also, there is a close relationship between the Governor and the Union Government. In 1980, there was Congress(I) Government at the Centre. 'Nine non-Congress(I) State Legislative Assemblies of Punjab, Haryana, Himachal Pradesh, Uttar Pradesh, Bihar, Madhya Pradesh, Rajasthan, Orissa and West Bengal were dissolved by the President of India on the advice of the Central Cabinet'.[21]

Governor's Power to Reserve a Bill Passed by State Legislature for the Consideration of the President

Article 200 of the Constitution of India gives the Governor of a State the power to reserve a bill passed by the State Legislature and refer it to the President for his consent. Every bill passed by Legislative Assembly or by the two Houses of the State Legislature (where there is the Legislative Council) comes to the Governor for his assent. The Governor, under the Article is constitutionally competent to reserve a bill passed by the State Legislature for the consideration of the President. Through this constitutional provision, the centre can interfere and control the affairs of the State. The President can give his assent to the bill or withhold his assent to the bill or return the bill to the house or houses which has already passed the bill for recommendation. The returned bill within a period of six months from the date of its receipt, is again passed with or without amendment within a week, then it shall be presented again to the President for his consideration. In such a way, the centre, through the President, can control the State Legislature.

Presidential Sanction over Certain Ordinances

The Constitution of India provides the Governor the power to promulgate ordinances in the recess of the State legislature. The Governor shall not promulgate ordinances without instructions from the President.[22]. Thus the Governors is in between the State Government and the Central Government. But the Governor, being appointed by the President, hold office during his pleasure, is in a very difficult position to go against the Central Government in exercising his discretionary power. The President can inform the State legislature through the Governor that such and such constitutional provision so reserved by the Governor for ordinance making is to be amended or dropped. Thus the State Governor really depends upon the Central Government in promulgating ordinances.

Union Control over State Administration

There are many provisions in the Constitution of India which empowers the Union Government to issue administrative directions to the State administration. In such cases, the President can supersede the working of the State Government. The Centre can interfere in the internal affairs of the State through the following articles of the Constitution:

(a) Article 256 mentions that the executive power of every State shall be so exercised as to ensure compliance with the laws made by Parliament and any existing laws which apply in that State and the executive power of the Union shall extend to the giving of such direction to a State as may appear to the Government of India to be necessary for that purpose.

(b) Article 257 provides that the executive power of every State shall be so exercised as not to impede and prejudice the exercise of the executive power of the Union. The executive power of the Union extends to the giving of such direction to a state.

(c) According to Article 339(2), the executive power of the Union extends to the giving of directions to State for the welfare of the Schedule Tribes.

(d) Article 350(a) of the Constitution gives the President the power to issue any direction to any State as he considers necessary for providing adequate facilities for the introduction of mother tongue at the primary stage of education to children belonging to linguistic minorities.

(e) Under Article 351 of the Constitution, it is the duty of the Union to promote the spread of the Hindi language to develop it so that it may serve as a medium of expression for all the elements of the composition culture of India, etc.

These articles show that the State governments need to ensure compliance with the Union laws in running administration in the State. Further Part XI of the Constitution dealing the relation between the Union and the State, enable the Central Government to superintend, direct and control the State government through the institution of the Governor. Again under Article 365 of the Constitution, the President has the power to issue directions to the State government if the latter cannot be carried on in accordance with the provision of the Constitution. For example, President Rule was imposed on 30th April, 1977 in the nine States of Northern India by dissolving the Legislative Assemblies. The nine States are Punjab, Haryana, Himachal Pradesh, Uttar Pradesh, Bihar, Madhya Pradesh, Rajasthan, Orissa and West Bengal. The Assemblies were dissolved on the plea that the State government cannot be carried on in accordance with the provision of the Constitution. The fact was that these steps were taken up due to the failure of the Congress party in the last Lok Sabha elections. Consequently, the newly formed Janata Government at the Centre recommended for President's Rule.[23] The reason giving by the Centre for dissolution of nine State Assemblies was that the voters did not want the Congress party not only in the Lok Sabha but also in the State Assemblies. Thus the functioning of the Government of these nine States was taken over by the President.

The Governor and the Failure of the Constitutional Machinery in the State

Part XVII of the Constitution of India covering from Article 352 to Article 360 contain emergency provisions. These provisions curtailed the autonomy of the State governments. The State Governor, under these articles, has to play a very important role, sometimes acting as a central agent to the State Governments. 'He is the link that fastens the federal State chain, the channel which regulates the Union and State relation'.[24] When the Government of a State does not function smoothly, the Governor sends report to the President. And while preparing report, the Governor is not bound to consult the Chief Minister or council of Ministers. So the Governor's report is not in the knowledge of the Chief Minister and the ministry. It is from the report of the Governor that the Central Government has to decide whether there should be President's Rule or not in a State. In actual practice, the Governors are totally led by the Home Minister. The Governors are helpless in these matters as he hold office during the pleasure of the President which indirectly means pleasure of the Prime Minister.

After knowing the political condition of Mrs. Janaki, the CCPA discussed on the 20th January, 1988 the political developments in Tamil Nadu, but the State Governor's report was not available then. The Tamil Nadu Assembly was dissolved and President Rule was imposed in the State on the 30th January, 1988 after getting the Governor's report from Mr. Khurana stating that 'Mrs. Janaki had failed to prove her majority in a legal and constitutional manner in the State Assembly. Since she had got only 99 votes in a House of 221 members, her government was in a minority'.[25]

Under Article 365 of the Constitution of India, the President has power to declare whether a situation has arisen in which the government of the State cannot be carried on in accordance with the provisions of the Constitution. Really it is the Governor who will inform the President whether there is failure of constitutional machinery in the State or not? The action of the President depends upon the report of the Governor of the State. That is why the Governor is regarded as the watch dog of the Centre. The Governor, being the watch dog of the Centre limited the autonomy of the State.

The Prime Minister, being the real head of the Centre also plays an important part in the relationship between the Centre and the State. In Jammu and Kashmir, the Governor Jagmohan submitted a 40 page report to the Prime Minister listing charges of corruption against Shah Ministry and his Cabinet shortly after the formation of the Ministry. It is believed that the Governor even threatened to resign unless the Government was dismissed and Governor's rule imposed."[26] Accordingly, the Shah Ministry was dismissed and the State was put under President's rule. Recently the weeklong political circle in Nagaland was solved by the imposition of President's Rule. The Governor General K.V. Krishna Rao in his report said, 'given the situation that arisen in Nagaland, the Government could not have worked in accordance with the provision of the Constitution."[27]

In this connection, the Nagaland opposition leader Vamuzo said, "The Governor has acted on the whims of the Congress(I) High Command rather exciting his constitutional responsibilities. Describing the imposition of President's Rule as an insult to the Nagas would not help solve any problem in this sensitive, insurgency afflicted State".[28]

V.V. Giri when he was the Governor of Mysore before his Presidentship of India 'called himself to be an ambassador of the Central Government to the State administration'.[29] It is more so during the period of President's Rule.

By knowing the close relationship between the centre and the Governor, Jyoti Basu, the Governor of West Bengal at a convention on the role of Governors organized by the All-India Lawyer' Union in New Delhi on the 8th April, 1989 said, "most Governors have played blatantly partisan roles as agents of New Delhi. They have helped assent to bills and dismissed democratic government without pretext. The Chief dismissed democratic government without pretext. The Chief Minister of Kerala and Karnataka E.K. Nayanar and S.R. Bommai along with Jyoti Basu alleged that the Congress(I)

Government at the Centre had turned the office of Governors into a political tool to destabilise opposition State government".[30]

MANIPUR

Before the coming of the institution of governorship in Manipur in 1972, the relation between the centre and the State of Manipur was very close. The relation was maintained through the Administrator under the Union Territories Act 1963. Although the Legislative Assembly under the Act was given some legislative and executive powers, the Administrator possessed immense powers. The Administrator was, in a true sense, the representative of the Central Government. Later on in December, 1969, the name of the head of the State was changed to Lieutenant Governor Baleswar Prasad and D.R. Kohli were Lieutenant Governors from 1969 to January, 1970 and from January, 1970 to January, 1972 respectively.

In January 1972, Manipur became a full fledged State of the Indian Union. Since then, the relationship between the Centre and the State of Manipur was conducted through the Governor. The relationship may be examined under the following heads:

Appointment of the Governor

Article 155 of the Constitution of India states that the Governor of a State shall be appointed by the President by warrant under his hand and seal. The first Governor of Manipur, B.K. Nehru was appointed by the President of India and joined the office of Governorship in Manipur on 21st January, 1972, the day of inauguration of statehood in Manipur by Prime Minister, Indira Gandhi. Before his appointment as Governor, B.K. Nehru was also the Governor of Assam, Meghalaya, Nagaland and Tripura. This factor (the Governor of the neighbouring States) might have promoted the President of India to appoint B.K. Nehru as Governor of Manipur. It may be remembered that there was no ministry in Manipur, at the time of the appointment of the Governor. The State was under President's Rule. The political parties and the people of Manipur were too happy to welcome B.K.

Nehru as Governor of Manipur. The second Governor, L.P. Singh become the head of State in Manipur on 12 August, 1973.[31] At the time of appointment of L.P Singh as Governor of the State, there was no ministry in the State. The State was under President's Rule due to the downfall of the MPP led coalition government led by Md. Alimuddin. The appointment was due to the change of Governorship of Assam, Meghalaya, Nagaland and Tripura as there was common Governor for these state including Manipur. S.M. Burney was the third Governor appointed by the President of India in Manipur. He joined the office of Governorship on 12 August, 1981. There was Congress Ministry in the State at the time of appointment. There was no conflict between the Centre and the State government at the appointment of S.M. Burney as Governor of the States. The retired General R.V. Krishna Rao became the head of State on 12th June, 1984. He was purely the choice of the Central Government, appointed by the President of India. The State government warmly welcome the appointment. The fifth and present Governor Chintamani Panigrahi was appointed by the President of India, R. Venkataraman. He joined the office of Governor on 10th of July, 1989. There was Congress ministry headed by R.K. Jaichandra Singh in the State. The Ministry welcomed the appointment very warmly.

Removal of Governor

The centrally appointed Governor of Manipur can be removed, transferred or changed by the Central Government. The Constitution of India under Article 156(1) provides that the Governor shall hold office during the pleasure of the President. It is a fact that the transfers and removal of Governors are being done in such a manner that instead of becoming personality above politics, they have become the political instruments for the fulfilment of the political schemes of the ruling party at the Centre Government.[32] The third Governor S.K. Burney, after the completion of one term was transferred by the Centre as the Governor of Haryana. Similarly, the fourth Governor Gen. K.V.

Krishna Rao (Retd.), after the completion of one term was transferred as the Governor of Jammu and Kashmir. Of all the Governors of Manipur, Lalan Prasad Singh hold the post of Governorship for longest period, i.e., more than nine years. The transfers of Governors from Manipur were purely done on the desire of Governors from Manipur were than nine years. The transfers of Governors from Manipur were purely done on the desire of the Central Government and not of the demand of the ministry or political parties or the people of Manipur.

Discretion of the Governor

The Governors of Manipur exercise their discretionary power in order to maintain a close relationship with the Centre. The role of the Governor in this aspect may be examined in three areas, i.e., (a) the appointment of the Chief Minister; (b) the dismissal of the Ministry; and (c) the prorogation and dissolution of the Legislative Assembly.

Appointment of the Chief Minister

In the Assembly elections of Manipur in 1972, no party secured majority. The Manipur Peoples' Party was able to get the support of 32 members. The Congress party also requested the Governor to allow the party to form the government. It may also remembered that the Congress was the ruling party at the Centre under the strong leadership of Indira Gandhi. The Governor B.K. Nehru physically verified the MLAs belonging to the United Legislature Party.[33] The Governor appointed Md. Alimuddin as Chief Minister of the State as the latter was the undisputed leader of the United Legislature Party. The same happened during the Governorship of L.P. Singh while he appointed Md. Alimuddin as the Chief Minister after the mid-term Assembly elections of 1974. The appointments of Yangmaso Shaiza of the Progressive Democratic Front and R.K. Dorendro of the Congress and United Legislature party coalition Ministry as Chief Ministers in July 1974 and December 1974 respectively was done purely on the exercise of the discretionary power independently by the Governor, L.P. Singh. In this case, the Governor was not guided by the Central Government.

During the long period from 1972 to 1990, there was only one case where the action of the Governor on the appointment of the Chief Minister was very much influenced by the Centre. That was in 1988 when Governor Gen. (Retd.) K.V. Krishna Rao appointed, R.K. Jaichandra was Minister of state in the Union Government. In spite of the claim of three leaders in the State Ministry, to be the Chief Minister of the State, the Central Government headed by Prime Minister Rajiv Gandhi asked the Governor to appoint R.K. Joichandra as Chief Minister of the State. Here the appointment was purely on the basics of the desire of the Central Government.

Dismissal of the Ministry

There was only one case of the dismissal of Ministry by the Governor. That was in 1979. There were many charges, e.g., deterioration of law and order in the State corruption, etc., against the Ministry. The opposition parties also urged the President N. Sanjiva Reddy and the Central leader to dismiss the Janata Ministry headed by Yangmaso Shaiza. The Governor, L.P. Singh dismissed the Ministry in spite of the claim of the Chief Minister that there was no Constitutional crisis and deterioration of law and order in the State. Here the action of the Governor was perhaps influenced by the Janata Government at the Centre.

Prorogation and Dissolution of the Assembly

In the prorogation and dissolution of the Manipur Legislative Assembly, the Governor of Manipur was not always influenced by the Central Government. For example, in March 1973 after the downfall of the MPP led coalition ministry, the Governor B.K. Nehru dissolved the Legislative Assembly. It may be remembered that the Congress(I) having the support of 32 members in a House of 60 was requesting the Governor to form the government. So the

Governor was not guided by the Central Congress(I) Government in dissolving the Legislative Assembly. The next was in 19 November, 1979. The Governor L.P. Singh dissolved the Legislative Assembly along with the dismissal of the Janata Ministry headed by Morarji Desai at the Centre.

Governor's Power to Reserve a Bill passed by the State Legislature for the consideration of the President

The Governor of Manipur sometimes reserve a bill passed by the Manipur Legislative Assembly for the consideration of the President thereby maintaining a close relation between the Central Government and the State Government. One such important instance was the reservation of the Manipur Official Language Bill 1978 by the Governor L.P. Singh for the consideration of the President. It was in March 1978 that the Manipur Legislative Assembly unanimously passed the Manipur Official Language Bill 1978, designating Manipuri 'written in Bengali script' as the official language of the State. The hill people are afraid that if the Manipur language, i.e., the language of the Meiteis is the official language of the State, they would be at a disadvantage and may be exploited. These factors influenced the Governor to reserve the Bill for the consideration of the President. So the President or the Central Government had time to examine the implications of the Bill in the interest of the State. The approval of the Bill by the President of the India pacify the hill people and they could understand the real situation of the State.

Presidential Sanction over Certain Ordinances

The Governor of Manipur promulgated about 27 Ordinances during the period from 1975 to 1983. For issuing certain ordinances, the Governor got sanction from the President of India. In these process, the role of the Governor is very important in bringing understanding between the Central Government headed by the President of India and the State Government headed by the Chief Minister of the State. So far there is no misunderstanding or conflict between the

Central Government and State government regarding the promulgation of ordinances.

Union Control over State Administration

The administration of the State of Manipur is very much controlled by the various provision of Union control over State administration given in the Constitution of India through the Governor. The administration of the State Government always ensured complaints with the Union laws, directions and advice given by the Central Government through the Governor from time to time. If the Governor thinks that the administration of the State cannot be carried on according to the provisions of the Constitution, the Central Government take over the administration of the State. The Governor carried on the administration as real head of the State. That was what happened in Manipur in March 1973, May 1977, November 1979 and February 1981. In these cases, the administration of the State was completely in the hands of the Central Government. Another example of Central control over State administration was regarding insurgencies. The State of Manipur suffers from insurgency from the latter part of 1970s. in framing and implementing policies to control and suppress insurgencies, the State administration, it may be said, comes under total control of the Union Government. The governor plays a very important part in this circumstances. The policies to promote the welfare of the scheduled tribes and other linguistic minorities are usually laid by the Union Government. The Governor as an agent of the Union Government has to see whether these policies are implemented by the State government.

The Governor of Manipur under Article 399(2) exercise his discretionary power by sanctioning every year a heavy amount in terms of crore for the development of the scheduled tribes in the State. In addition, he also persues the Central Government for many schemes and programmes for tribal development under the centrally sponsored heads. Mention may be made for example "under the special Central Assistance, an amount of ₹ 824.00 lakhs has been provided during the Sixth Five Year Plan period, 1980-85, of which an amount of ₹ 130.00 lakhs, 149.00 lakhs, 169.00 lakhs were earmarked for the year, 1980-81 1981-82 and 1982-83 respectively. During the year under report the sector for the implementation of various developmental programmes in the hill areas of Manipur".[34] In a adition to those "a few centrally sponsored schemes are also implemented for Scheduled Castes and Scheduled Tribes on 50 : 50 basis between the Centre and the State".[35]

The Governor and the Failure of Constitutional Machinery in the State

The politics of Manipur was characterised by immense degree of political instability during the period from 1972 to 1977. The Governor had to see whether the administration of the State could be run according to the provisions of the Constitution. It was on the basis of the report sent by the Governor that the Central Government had to decide to impose or not to impose President's Rule in the State. It was on the basis of the Governor B.K. Nehru that the President of India imposed President's Rule in Manipur in March 1973 on the ground that the administration of the State could not be carried on in accordance with the provision of the Constitution. It may be remembered that the progressive Democratic Alliance led by the Congress(I) having the support of 32 members requested the Governor to allow them to form the government. But the Governor recommended the imposition of President's Rule. The same happened in May 1977 when the Governor L.P. Singh recommended the suspension of the legislative Assembly and imposition of President's Rule in the State when the Congress ministry led by R.K. Dorendro Singh resigned due to the defection of a large number of Congress MLAs to Janata Party. Accordingly the President suspended the Legislative Assembly and imposed President's Rule in the State. Thus the relation between the Union Government and the Governor was very close. The only instance where the Union Government did not accept the recommendation of the Governor was in February 1989. The Governor Chintamani Panigrahi recommended the imposition of President's Rule on the

State when the Congress(I) ministry led by R.K. Joichandra Singh completed its term. But contrary to the recommendation of the Governor, the Union Government allowed R.K. Jaichandra's Ministry as a caretaker government.[36] It was not due to a conflict between the Union Government and the Governor. The newly formed National Front Government under the Prime Ministership of V.P. Singh perhaps wanted to show a gesture to the Congress(I) Government in the State.

The role of the Governor of Manipur in maintaining the relationship between the Union Government and the State Government is important. Manipur being a very small State of the Indian Union is very easily influenced by the politics of the Centre. That was what happened in 1977 when the Janata Party came to power in the Centre. Within a very short period, Manipur witnessed the formation of a Janata Ministry in the State (first in India) by means of defection from the Congress party which had the majority support of more than 50 members in the House of 60. After the Assembly elections of January 1990 again the opposition parties led by MPP was able to form the United Front Government under the Chief Ministership of R.K. Ranabir Singh mainly due to the newly formed National Front Government at the Centre. In such circumstances the Governor of Manipur has to see whether the State government acts in tune with the Union Government, being the appointee of the Union Government as well as the head of the State of Manipur. The Governor can interfere in order to resolve a crisis or a conflict between the Centre and the State.

References

1. Meera Shrivastava, *Constitutional Crisis in the States in India.* Concept Publishing Company, New Delhi, 1980, pp. 88-89.
2. Durga Das, *Indira from Curzon to Nehru and After,* James Place, London, 1959, p. 337.
3. *Parliamentary Debates*, November 15, 1967, p. 796.
4. *Constituent Assembly Debate*, Vol. VIII, p. 471.
5. N. Sanajaoba, (ed), *Basic Isues on Centre-State Relations,* Omsons Publication, Guwahati, 1985, p. 91.

6. *Constituent Assembly Debate*, Vol. VIII, Lok Sabha Secretariat, New Delhi, p. 471.
7. Gehlot, N.S., *The Office of the Governor*, Chugh Publication, Allahabad, 1977, p. 34.
8. *The Statesman* (Calcutta), 10-4-1967.
9. *Ibid.*, 28.5.1967.
10. Gehlot, N.S., *The Federalism, Framework of Indian Politics*, Gitabali Publishing House, New Delhi, 1983, p. 124.
11. *The Telegrah*, 2.2.1990.
12. *Ibid.*, 9.2.1988.
13. *Constituent Assembly Debate*, *op. cit.* p. 73.
14. The *Statesmen*, Calcutta, 8-8-1981.
15. The *Amrita Bazar Patrika*, 22-9-1981.
16. *The Telegraph*, 16-1-1990.
17. Khanna, N.R., 'Delhi's Men in States; Preserving Confidence in Governors', *Statesman* (Calcutta), 5-2-1990.
18. *The Telegraph*, 29-1-1990.
19. *Times of India*, 15-1-1982.
20. *Huyen Lalpao*, 5-8-1988.
21. *Simanta Patrika*, 8-2-1980.
22. Article 213(1), *The Constitution of India*.
23. The *Simanta Patrika*, 3-5-1977.
24. Rao, N. Rang, 'The Governor and the State', *Times Weekly*, Vol. 3, No. 5, New Delhi, September 10, 1972.
25. *The Telegraph*, 30-1-1988.
26. Tavlun Singh, "Tale of two Governors', *The Governor, Rage and Saboteur*. Roli Books International, New Delhi, 1980, p. 145.
27. *The Telegraph*, 8-8-1988.
28. The *Amrita Bazar Patrika*, 9-8-1988.
29. *The Hindustan Times*, 9-12-1960.
30. *The Telegraph*, 9-4-1989.
31. Government of Manipur Administrative Report, Imphal 1973.
32. Sati Shahni (ed), *Centre State Relations*, Vikas Publishing House, New Delhi, 1984, p. 10.
33. The Gokul Singh, *Defection in Manipur*, 1963-1977, Imphal, 1979, pp. 40-41.
34. *Annual Administrative Report*, 1983-84 for the Tribal Development, Manipur, Imphal, p. 2.
35. *Ibid.*
36. *The Poknapahm*, 19-2-1990.

CHAPTER-VII

Conclusion

The role of the Governor as representative of the Centre is very important in the politics of India. The role is very significant from the part of national integration and further preservation of national standards in public administration. Such role is not received enough recognition by any other administrative organ of the Centre. As an agent of the Centre to the State he has to keep the Centre informed about the affairs of the State which can endanger the unity and integrity of the country. For this purpose he sends fortnightly reports to the President without any knowledge of the Council of Ministers.

For the proper functioning of a strong federation and maintenance of healthy Centre-State relation, the role of the Governor becomes with every change in the political map of India when the Centre and State are not ruled by the same political party. From the prevailing political context in India, "the former supreme Court Judge, Justice V.R. Krishna Iyer has described the practice of changing Governors in the State with the change of Government at the Centre and described it as 'experiments in political pollution and trafficking in Governorship'. He has accused the former Prime Minister, Mrs. Indira Gandhi and Mr. Rajiv Gandhi of violating the Constitutional norms in appointing Governors".[1]

Recently in the two days Annual Conference of Governors at New Delhi from 27 and 28 July, 1990 the Governors were of the view that "the grievances of the people specially the economic problems of the poorest sections of the society including Scheduled Castes and Scheduled Tribes should be addressed on priority basis.

They also gave a brief resumé of the political, law and order and economic situation in the State and felt that the problem of unemployment needed to be given top priority".[2]

As head of the State the role of the Governor is important. He is the legislative head, executive head, judicial head and financial head. He has also to play a very significant role in the State public services and in the University or Universities of the State as Chancellor.

The Governor of Manipur enjoys his roles as the legislative head, executive head, judicial head, and financial head. In the Manipur State Public Services, the Governor performs his administrative functions satisfactorily. He is also the Chancellor of the Manipur University having the Legislative Power, Executive Power, Judicial Power and Financial Power as provided by the Manipur University Act.

Being the head of the State, the Governor of Manipur has a special responsibility for the tribal people of the State. The Tribal Development and Welfare Department of Manipur takes the responsibility for promoting the welfare of the tribal people. The Governor of Manipur tries to promote the State oriented schemes, the Centre-State oriented Schemes and the Centre oriented schemes for the Scheduled Caste and Scheduled Tribe peoples of the State.

The Governor is an integral part of the State legislature. His role in the Legislative process of the State by having the power to nominate members to the legislature, summing the Legislative Assembly, proroguing and dissolving the Assembly of the State cannot be underestimated. He also gives address to the Assembly, issues Ordinances in the State, assents to the bills passed by the State Legislature and sometimes sends messages to the Legislature.

The Governor of Manipur plays his legislative role in the functioning of the State administration (except the nomination of members to the State legislature). Under the Rules of Procedure and Conduct of Business of the Manipur Legislative Assembly, the Governor can summon, prorogue and dissolve the Legislative Assembly. He gives his address in the Assembly by mentioning many developmental programmes to be performed in the State.

Being the head of the State, the Governor takes the oath of every newly elected MLAs after every Assembly election. He also issues ordinances when the Assembly is not in session. The Governor gives his assent to the bills to become an Act and sometimes he returns the bill to the House for reconsideration. Thus he has a great relation with the State legislature.

The relation between the Governor and the Council of Ministers is very important and significant as the ministers hold office during the pleasure of the Governor. He appoints the Chief Minister of the Council of Minister. Regarding the expansion of the ministry he has a final voice as he has to take oath of newly appointed minister though their names are recommended by the Chief Minister. The Chief Minister has sometimes to act according to the desire of the Governor. It is in the interest of both the Governor and the Chief Minister to have a close relation between the two.

In Manipur, the Governor has a very significant role in the appointment of the members, of the ministers, of the council of ministers specially in the appointment of the Chief Minister. In the State, no political party secures absolute majority for the formation of a State ministry after almost every Assembly election since 1972. The Governor can invite the leader of the single largest majority party or the leader of the second largest majority party to form the Government. Regarding the size of the Ministry also he advised the concerned Chief Minister to limit the size on a reasonable basis. Sometimes it happened that there was no arrangement for oath taking ceremony at Raj Bhavan when the member of the Legislative Assembly come to the Raj Bhavan for taking oath as ministers for the expansion of the ministry. It shows that the Chief Minister could not expand his ministry without getting the approval from the Governor.

The Governor exercises his discretionary power in the following matters, such as (i) The appointment of the Chief Minister, (ii) Dismissal of the Chief Minister/Ministry, (iii) Summoning of the State Legislative Assembly, (iv) Proroguing the sitting of the State Legislative Assembly, (v) Dissolution of the State Legislature, (vi) In getting or seeking of information from the Chief Minister on both the legislative and administrative matter, (vii) In giving assent to the bills passed by the State Legislature or in returning the bills, (viii) Reservation of bills for the consideration of the President, (ix) promulgation of Ordinances, (x) Reporting to the President regarding the breakdown of the Constitutional machinery in the State under Article 356, (xi) in exercise the special power given under the Sixth Schedule of the Constitution of India, and (xii) the exercise of power under Article 371 of the Constitution of India.

The Governors of Manipur since 1972 had been exercising the discretionary power in the relevant matters like the Governors of other states. In 1975, the Governor L.P. Singh exercised his discretion by advising R.K. Dorendro to form the Government after taking personal verification of 3 MLAs who were in the rival camp of Yangmaso Shaiza. In 1988 also the Governor General K.V. Krishna Rao (Retd.) in the midst of dissident politics within the Congress(I) party appointed the former Union Minister of State R.K. Jaichandra as Chief Minister of the State.

The Governor also exercised discretionary power in dismissing the Ministry. The Governor L.P. Singh dismissed the Janata Ministry in 1979 which caused President's rule in Manipur. In summoning the State Legislature, proroguing the Assembly, dissolving the Assembly, etc., the Governor of Manipur exercised his discretion.

At his discretion, the Governor has given his assent to the bills passed by the State Legislature or sometimes returned the bills, reserved some bills for the consideration of the President under Article 356, exercised special powers under the Sixth Schedule and under Article 371 of the Constitution of India.

The successful working of the Indian federation, it may be said, is due to the existence of the institution of the Governor. The Central Government can easily control the State governments of India through the Governors in matters like the appointment of the Governor, removal of the Governor, taking part in exercising the discretionary power of the Governor, Governor's power to reserve bill passed by the State Legislature for the consideration of the President, Presidential sanction over certain ordinances and in reporting about the failure of the constitutional machinery of the State by the Governor.

The Governor of Manipur also brings the administration of Manipur in close relationship with the Central Government. The appointments and removals of all the five Governors of the State from 1972 onwards were done by the President of India under the provisions of the Constitution of India. The Governor of Manipur exercised his discretion in the appointment and removal of the Chief Minister of the State. He also dismissed the Ministry, prorogued the Assembly sittings, dissolved the Assembly, reserved the bills passed by the State Legislature for the consideration of the President and promulgated certain ordinances at his discretion for maintaining a close relationship with the Central Government. The Union Government also keeps good relationship through various provisions of the Constitution with the Government of Manipur.

There are many suggestions from different political experts, term, commission, etc., regarding the appointment and the role of the Governor. Regarding the appointment of the Governor, the Sarkaria Commission recommended that the Prime Minister should be consulted confidentially and informally the Vice President and the Speaker of the Lok Sabha and also the Chief Minister of the State should also be consulted. For this purpose, the provision under Article 155 which merely says that "the Governor of a State shall be appointed by the President by warrant under his hand and seal may be amended"[3] the Commission also suggested that the person to be appointed as he:

(1) should be eminent in some walk of life;
(2) should be a person from outside the State;
(3) should be a detached figure and not too intimately connected with local parties of the State; and
(4) should be a person who has not taken too great a part in politics".[4]

It can also be suggested that the Governor of a State should not be changed with the change of every ruling power at Centre. The Sarkaria Commission suggested that in order to ensure security of tenure, 5 years term of the Governor should not be disturbed except very rarely. In the present context of the politics of India, the tenure of the Governors very much depend upon the tenure of the ruling party at the Centre.

Regarding the relation between the Governor and the Centre, it may be suggested that in every action the Governor is not to be guided by the Centre. He should also exercise his power as the head of the State in spite of being a central agent. He has to discharge his State functions independently of the Central advice.

It may further be suggested that in exercising discretion the Governor should not be influenced by the Centre. As a matter of fact, the discretionary power so far exercised by the Indian Governors are not their personal decision but mainly the opinion of the Prime Minister of India or the Home Minister which is partial or one sided. Encouraging this statement, the former President of India V.V. Giri said, "The Governors cannot obviously base their actions on threats and fears. Their business is to see that they function strictly within the four corners of the Constitution according to their best judgement and ability in the interest of the people when they are pledged to serve".[5]

The Administrative Reform Commission also recommended that "guidelines should be formulated by the Inter-State Council and on acceptance by the Union issued in the name of the President".[6]

It may always be in the mind of the Governor that there is always a difference between the interest of the people of the State and the interest of the ruling political party at the Centre. In short, we can say that the Union and State relationship which is very important for preserving federal principle, to a large extent depends upon the Governor, his personality, and his role in the working of the political system of India.

References

1. *The Telegraph*, 29-1-1990.
2. *Ibid.*, 28-7-1990.
3. *Ibid.*, 9-2-1988.
4. *Ibid.*
5. *The Statesman*, 14-2-1969.
6. Administrative Reforms Commission Report, 1967, New Delhi, p. 25.

APPENDIX-I

List of Governors in Manipur

Sl. No.	Name	Took Office	Left Office
1.	B. K. Nehru	21 January 1972	20 September 1973
2.	LP. Singh	21 September 1973	11 August 1981
3.	S.M.H. Burney	18 August 1981	11 June 1984
4.	K.V. Krishna Rao	12 June 1984	7 July 1989
5.	Chintamani Panigrahi	10 July 1989	19 March 1993
6.	K.V. Ragnunatha Reddy	20 March 1993	30 August 1993
7.	V.K. Nayar	31 August 1993	22 December 1994
8.	O.N. Srivastava	23 December 1994	11 February 1999
9.	Ved Marwah	2 December 1999	12 June 2003
10.	Arvind Dave	13 June 2003	5 August 2004
11.	Shivinder Singh Sidhu	6 August 2004	22 July 2008
12.	Gurubachan Jagat	23 July 2008	22 July 2013
13.	Ashwani Kumar	23 July 2013	31 December 2013
14.	Vmod Duggal	31 December 2013	25 August 2014
15.	K.K. Paul (Addl Charge)	16 Sept 2014	

APPENDIX-II

List of Chief Ministers in Manipur

1. F.F. Pearson, July 1947 to August 1947.
2. M.K. Priyobrata Singh, August 1947 to October 1949.
3. Shri M. Koireng Singh, July 1963 to October 1967.
4. Shri L. Thambou Singh, October 1967 to October 1967.
5. Shri M. Koireng Singh, February 1968 to October 1969.
6. Md. Alimuddin, March 1972 to March 1973.
7. Md. Alimuddin, March 1974 to July 1974.
8. Mr. Yangmaso Shaiza, July 1974 to December 1974.
9. Shri R.K. Dorendro Singh, December 1974 to May 1977.
10. Mr. Yangmaso Shaiza, June 1977 to November 1979.
11. Shri R.K. Dorendro Singh, January 1980 to November 1980.
12. Mr. Rishang Keishing, November 1980 to February 1981.
13. Mr. Rishang Keishing, June 1981 to January 1985.
14. Mr. Rishang Keising, January 1985 to March 1988.
15. Shri R.K. Jaichandra, March 1988 to February 1990.
16. Shri R.K. Ranbir Singh, February 1990 to January, 1992.
17. Shri R.K. Dorendro Singh, April 1992 to December 1993.
18. Mr. Rishang Keishing, December 1994 to February 1995.
19. Mr. Rishang Keishing, February 1995 to December 1997.
20. Shri W. Nipamacha, December 1997 to March 2000.
21. Shri W. Nipamacha, March 2000 to February 2001.
22. Shri Radhabinod Koijam, February 2001 to May 2001.
23. Shri O. Ibobi, March 2002 to March 2007.
24. Shri O. Ibobi, 14th March 2007 till date.

APPENDIX-III

Manipur State Constitution Act 1947

Whereas it is expedient to enact a law for the governance of the Manipur State, His Highness the Maharaja of Manipur is pleased to enact as follows:

Chapter I

1. *Title:* This Act shall be called the Manipur State Constitution Act 1947.
2. *Extent and Application:* This Act shall extend to the whole of the Manipur State inclusive of the Hill Areas saying that it shall not apply in any matter where a specific reservation of powers is made to any authority in the Hills under the provisions of the Manipur State Hill People's (Administration) Regulation 1947.
3. *Government of the State by His Highness the Maharajah:* The territories for the time being and hereafier vested in the Maharajah are governed by and in the name of the Maharajah. All rights, authority and jurisdiction which appertain or are incidental to the Government of such territories are exercisable by the Maharajah subject to the provision of this Act.
4. *Succession:* Succession to the throne shall be governed by the Law of Primogeniture provided that the heir must be the legitimate son of a marriage recognised by the Council of Ministers. In the event of failure of heirs in the

direct male line, His Highness the Maharajah shall, after consultation with the Council of Ministers and the Assembly, designate his heir.

5. *Attainment of Majority:* The Maharajah or his heir shall be taken to attain majority at the age of 21 years.
6. *Council of Regency:*
   (a) Where by reason of the Maharajah being a minor or where by reason of any mental defect or grave bodily sickness as a result of which the Maharajah becomes permanently incapable of exercising his powers, the Council of Ministers shall take steps to set up a Council of Regency which shall exercise those powers in the State and shall continue in office for such time as the Council may determine;
   (b) Notwithstanding the provisions of sub-sections (a) above, the Maharajah in consultation with the Council of Ministers may, at any time or for any reason which may appear suitable, set up a Council of Regency to exercise his functions;
   (c) A Council of Regency set up under sub-section (a) and (b) above, may comprise of one or more persons may seem desirably, the Regent or Council of Regency shall before taking office be required to take an oath before the State Assembly to be loyal to the State and to observe faithfully its Constitution and laws;
   (d) Where in any event it shall be necessary to set up a Council of Regency either for the reasons laid down in sub-sections (a) and (b) above or for any other reason or where for any reason the Maharajah has become incapable of exercising his powers before such Regency can be set up, the Council of Ministers shall take whatever steps may be necessary for the governance of the State till such time as the Regency is created.
7. *Failure of Heirs and Disputed Succession:*
   (a) In the event of failure of heirs in the direct male line

and failure of the Maharajah to designate his heir under Section 4 above, a joint extraordinary session of the State Assembly and the Council of Ministers shall immediately be convened and shall remain in closed and continuous session till it shall have determined by a 75 per cent majority of the members present and voting, the persons to whom the throne shall pass;

(b) Where for any reason the succession to the throne is disputed, the Council of Ministers shall, on the death of the Ruler, take such steps as may immediately be necessary for the good governance of the State and shall refer the matter under dispute to the Chief Court for decision. Where any party is aggrieved by the decision of the Chief Court, an appeal shall lie to such authority as may be determined hereafter.

8. *The Maharajah's Prerogatives*

(a) All family matters which are the Maharaja's sole concern as head of the ruling family, all matters which are his sole concern as the defender of faith and all matters connected with titles. Honours and palace ceremonial shall be deemed to fall within the Maharajah's personal prerogative and in such matters the Maharajah shall exercise full discretion subject to the provisions of the Constitution and law of the State. The Maharajah's prerogative shall not, however, be taken to comprise any matter wherein the legitimate interests of the State administrations or civil right sustainable in a court of law is involved. It will be within the prerogative of the Maharajah to remit punishment and pardon offenders subject to the provisions of the Manipur State Court's Act provided that this prerogative shall not prejudice the right of any individual to compensation;

(b) It shall be the prerogative of the Maharajah and the Maharani that neither may be made answerable at law or subject to any legal proceeding in the State Courts. Their persons and property shall be inviolable;

(c) Notwithstanding Section 8(b) above, it shall be lawful for the State Council in consultation with the Chief Court to draw up a statement of charges against the Maharajah or the Maharani where it is proved beyond all possible doubt that the Maharajah or the Maharani has been guilty or murder or any other heinous offence or of any extreme political crime against the provisions of the Constitution;

(d) On a statement of charges being drawn up under clause (c) above, the Council shall present it before the Maharajah or the Maharani and require satisfaction. Should satisfaction be not forthcoming the Council may refer the matter to such authority as may be determined hereafter.

Chapter II

9. Definitions

In this Act and Rules issued thereunder unless there is something repugnant to the subject or the context:

(a) State shall mean the Manipur State comprising the whole territory of Manipur as delineated in the maps of the Survey of India current at the date of this enactment.

(b) The Maharajah means His Highness the Maharajah of Manipur, the Constitutional Head of this enactment.

(c) Chief Minister means the office entrusted with the chief executive function of the State.

(d) Minister means a member of the Council of Ministers appointed under this Act by name or by virtue of his office to administer certain branches of the State administration and to perform the duties and exercise the power imposed and conferred upon a minister by this Act and Rules framed thereunder.

(e) Council means the State Council of Ministers constituted under this Act.

(f) Gazette means the official journal of the State by means of which important orders, notices communiques, etc., are published.

(g) Speaker means the President of the Assembly and includes the Deputy Speaker in the absence of the Speaker or in the absence of both, a member voted to the chair.

(h) Civil List means the appropriation of funds for the expenses of the ruling family and the privy purse of the ruler.

(i) Privy purse means such portion of the Civil List as is appropriated exclusively for the personal expenses of the Maharajah.

(j) Revenue includes all receipts of the State from State assets, from all lands, forest, taxes, fines, penalties, forfeitures, lapses and other sources.

(k) Rules means any rule issued under this Act.

(1) Fundamental rights shall mean those rights which the State people shall enjoy as of right under this Act.

(m) The pronoun 'he' and its derivatives are used for any person whether male or female.

Chapter III

The Executive

10. *Council of Ministers*

(a) Subject to the provisions of this Act and subject also to the provisions of the Rules for the Administration of the Manipur State, the executive authority of the State is delegated to and shall vest in the Council of Ministers.

(b) Where under this Act or the Rules for the Administration of the State, it is requisite that the approval of the Maharajah shall be taken to any measure, the Chief Minister shall seek the approval of the Maharajah in person or in writing and shall obtain the Maharajah's orders thereon. Should in any case the Maharajah's approval be withheld, the Maharajah shall be pleased to inform the Chief Minister in person or in writing and to communicate his reasons for withholding such approval in writing to the Council.

(c) The Council of Ministers shall consist of the Chief Minister and six other Ministers.

(d) The six Ministers on the Council shall be elected by the State Assembly subject to the provision that two of these Ministers shall be representatives of the hill people of the State elected in such manner as shall be laid down in the Rules of Business of the State Assembly.

(e) The Chief Minister shall be appointed by the Maharajah in consultation with the elected Ministers of the Council.

(f) The Chief Minister shall receive letters of appointment over the seal of Maharajah.

(g) The Chief Minister in consultation with the Ministers shall allot portfolios.

11. The Chief Minister shall be President of the Council and the Vice President shall be appointed by the Council.
12. The Council of Ministers shall have a common seal and shall be jointly responsible to the Maharajah for the administration of the State.
13. The Council of Ministers and the Ministers individually shall exercise such powers and functions as may be assigned to them by or under this Act or under the Rules for the Administration of the State.
14. The quorum necessary for the transaction of business at a meeting of the Council shall not be less than three excluding the President.
15. The Chief Minister and Ministers shall, on taking office,

swear an oath of loyalty and allegiance to the Maharajah in the following form:

> 'I (name of the Minister) having been appointed as a Member of the Manipur State Council, do solemnly swear that I will be loyal and faithful and bear true allegiance to the Maharajah, his heirs and successors and that I will faithfully discharge the duties laid on me under this Act.'

16. A Minister of the Council shall not be removable from office except in accordance with the provisions of Chapter IV below.

Chapter IV

17. There shall be constituted a State Assembly. The Assembly shall be elected for a period of three years and shall comprise representatives freely elected by the people on an adult franchise and on the principle of joint electorate. Elections shall be in such manner and by such franchise as may be laid down under the rules for the elections to the State Assembly provided always that the representatives returnable from General, Hill and Mohammedan Constituencies shall be in the ratios of 30 : 18 : 3 respectively with an additional two seats for the representatives or educational and commercial interests.
18. The State Assembly may debate all matters concerning the Government and well-being of the State which, in the opinion of five members of the Assembly, it is in the public interest to debate. The Assembly shall tender such advice to the Council of Ministers in any matter in which a majority of the members present, are agreed on the advice which shall be tendered provided that no matter touching the Maharajah's prerogative shall be debated and provided that the Maharajah may on the advice of the Council, veto

debate on any matter where such course shall in the public interest be necessary.

19. The State Assembly shall not tender advice to the Council on any matter which is of primary concern to the hill people unless such advice has the support of a majority of the hill representatives in the Assembly.
20. Subject to the provisions of this Act, the Assembly may make rules for regulating its proceedings and the conduct of business.
21. Where in any case it is required to pass a vote of no confidence against a minister of the Council for his individual acts, a motion of no confidence, signed by not less than ten members of the Assembly and laying out in detail, the facts giving rise to the motion, may with the permission of the Speaker of the Assembly be moved. If such motion shall receive the support of at least 75 per cent of the members present and voting, it shall be forwarded through the Chief Minister to the Maharajah, who, unless there appears strong and valid reasons to the contrary which shall be recorded in writing, shall after consultation with the Chief Minister require the Minister against whom the motion has been passed to resign.
22. Where in any case the State Council or the Maharajah is in the special circumstances of any case unable to accept the advice of the Assembly, the Maharajah or the State Council as the case may be, shall communicate in writing the reasons which have led to such course and shall give facilities for personal discussion of the matter with a representatives deputed by the Assembly.
23. Subject to the provisions of this Act and the rules framed under it for the disposal of the Assembly business, there shall be freedom of speech in the Assembly and no member shall be liable to any proceedings in any court in respect of any speech or vote given by him in the Assembly or a committee thereof and no person shall be liable in respect

of any publication by or under the authority of the Assembly of any report, paper, vote or proceedings.

24. No member of the Assembly shall be liable to arrest or detention in prison under a civil process: (a) if he is a member of the Assembly, during the continuance of the Assembly; and (b) if he is member of any committee of the Assembly, during the continuance of the meeting of the committee.
25. The elected Minister, the Speaker, Deputy Speaker and members of the Assembly shall receive such emoluments as may be determined from time to time by the Assembly.

Chapter V

The Law Making Authority

26. The Law Making Authority in the State shall consist of the Maharajah in Council in collaboration with the State Assembly acting under section 18 above.
27. When the Council or the Assembly consider that a law should be enacted the Council shall cause a bill to be drafted, which shall be laid before the Assembly and a reasonable time shall be given for consideration thereof. The Council then cause to be made such alternations or amendments as may be deemed necessary in the light of the advice tendered by the Assembly and the Chief Minister shall submit the Bill in its final form for the assent of the Maharajah.
28. On the receipt of the Maharajah's assent the Bill shall be published in the State Gazette and shall become an Act having the force of law.
29. Should the Maharajah in any case withhold his assent to a Bill, the Bill shall lapse as it had not been passed. If the assent of the Maharajah is not forthcoming within one calendar month of the Bill being submitted to him he shall be deemed to have withheld his assent.

30. Where the assent of Maharajah to any Bill is withheld, the Council may cause the self same Bill to be introduced in the next session of the Assembly and if passed without amendment by a 75 per cent majority of the Assembly, the Bill shall be certified over the Seal of the Council and shall become Law.
31. Nothing in this Chapter shall be deemed to derogate from the absolute right of the Maharajah in Council to promulgate, the emergency cases, orders having the force of law without previous reference to the Assembly where the public interest in their opinion demand that such order shall be promulgated provided that the first opportunity shall be taken of laying the order before the Assembly for consideration. Any such order shall not have the force of law for a period of more than six months.

Chapter VI

Finance

32. The revenue of the State and such other receipts as may accrue from whatever source, less such reasonable percentage of the total real revenue as may be reserved for the Civil List, are placed at the disposal of the Council for expenditure on the Government of the State in the manner prescribed by State Account Rules saving that in every year a sum represents not less than 17 per cent of the average real revenue of the State for the proceeding three years shall be allocated for expenditure on the welfare and administration of the hill people.
33. The Minister in-charge of finance shall prepare an annual budget showing the estimated receipts and expenditure for the ensuing year classified under the prescribed heads of account and shall submit it to the Assembly within fifteen days of its meeting for the budget session along with a statement of account for the previous year.

34. The Assembly shall after considering the budget, submit it with their recommendation to the Council, who, having made such modification as may be deemed necessary shall submit it to the Maharajah for approval. Where any delay occurs in the granting of assent to the budget by the Maharajah and where such assent has not been obtained by the first day of the financial year, provisional effect shall be given to the budget as passed by the Assembly and funds shall be drawn against its provisions as it had received assent.

35. The Maharajah's Civil List shall be fixed at a figure equal to 10 per cent of the real revenue of the State over the preceding three years, provided that no extraordinary revenues shall be taken into account when determining this amount and provided that no State revenue in excess of rupees twenty lakhs shall be taken into account in any one year. The appropriations to the Maharajah's Civil List shall be non-votable and shall not be the subject of debate in the Assembly.

36. No tax whatsoever shall be shown in the budget and no tax shall be collected by any officer of the State or by any person unless such tax has been imposed by due process of law.

37. (a) There shall be a State Auditor who shall be appointed by the Maharajah in Council on a nomination to be made by the Comptroller of Audit. Assam, or such other officer as may as deemed suitable. Such nominee shall be employed on contract for a period of not less than five years and shall be removed only by the Maharajah in Council in consultation with the Authority making the nomination.

(b) The conditions of services of the State Auditor shall be such as may be prescribed by the Maharajah in Council provided always that he shall not be eligible for any office of profit in the State after his retirement.

(c) The Auditor shall exercise such powers and perform

such duties as may be laid down in the State Account Rules.

Chapter VII

Hill People

38. The Council shall be responsible for the welfare and good administration of the hill people of the State and shall provide such funds for this purpose as may, subject to the provisions of Section 32 above, be deemed necessary, provided that the local authorities, in the hill shall exercise such powers of local self government as my be laid down in the Manipur State Hill (Administration) Regulation 1947.

Chapter VIII

The Services

39. The Council shall issue rules regulating the conditions of services in the departments of the State.
40. A Manipur State Appointments Board shall be constituted and the Council shall issue rule regulating the constitution, functions and procedure of the Board. The Board shall consist of not less than three members, one of whom must be a hill man and a chairman and shall be the final authority in all matters connected with appointments and promotions to the State service except in so far as specific powers may be reserved under this Act or the Rules for Administration of the State.

Chapter IX

The Judicature

41. (a) There shall be a complete separation of Judiciary from the Executive.

(b) The Judicature of the State shall be as laid down in the Manipur State Courts Act 1947.

42. The Chief Justice of the State and two Puisne Judges shall be appointed by the Maharajah in Council under the Royal Seal and shall hold office until the age of 65 years provided that:

(a) A judge may resign his office.

(b) A judge may be removed from his office by the Maharajah in Council only on the grounds of misbehaviour or infirmity of body or mind.

43. A person shall not be appointed as a Judge of the Chief Court unless he: (a) be a graduate in law and has held judicial office at least for five years; or (b) is a barrister qualified in England of five years' standing; or (c) has for at least five years held judicial office in British India in a post not inferior to that of a subordinate judge; or (d) has for at least a period of ten years been a pleader of any High Court or of the Manipur Chief Court; or (e) be a person recognised as having a special capacity for the exercise of judicial functions.

Chapter X

Fundamental Rights and Duties of Citizens

44. All citizens shall be equal before the law. Titles and other privileges of birth shall not be recognised in the eyes of the law.

45. The liberty of the individual shall be guarantee. No person may be subjected to any judicial interrogation or placed under arrest or be in any other way deprived of his liberty, save as provided by law.

46. No person shall be tried save by a competent court.

47. No person may be tried except by a competent court who shall give full opportunity to such person to defend himself by all legal means.

48. All penalties shall be as determined by law.
49. Capital punishment may not be inflicted for purely political crimes.
50. No citizens may be banished from the State, expelled from one part of the country to another and obliged to reside in a specified place save in such cases as may be expressly determined by law.
51. Every dwelling shall be inviolable save under express provision of law.
52. There shall be guaranteed to all people, justice, social, economic and political; equality of status, of opportunity and before the law; freedom of thought, expression of belief faith, worship, vocation, association, and action, subject to law and public morality.
53. The practice of Arts and Science shall be unrestricted and shall enjoy the protection and support of the State.
54. Without any prejudice to the communities concerned, public institutions shall be opened to all citizens of the States.
55. (a) All officials of the State or of a local government shall be answerable before the law for their individual and unlawful actions.
    (b) Where damage is caused to an individual by the act of an official of the State or an official of a local government, such individual may use the State before the Chief Court and may *bona fide* act of a State servant in pursuance of a policy duly laid down by a competent authority.

Chapter XI

General Clauses

56. Any provision of this act may be subject to amendment by the Maharajah in Council provided that such amendment is laid before the Assembly and receives the support of at least 80 per cent of the members of the State Assembly present at voting, when such amendment is debated.

57. Where in any case circumstances arise which prevent the proper operation in law or in spirit of this Constitution Act, the Council may at their discretion refer the matter for decision to such authority outside the State as may be decided hereafter and the decision of that authority shall be binding.
58. The Court Language of the State shall be Manipuri or English.

Bodha Chandra Singh
(Maharajah of Manipur)

APPENDIX-IV

Treaty of Yandaboo–February 24, 1826

Article No. 1

There shall be perpetual peace and friendship between the Honourable Company on the one part, and His Majesty the King of Ava on the other.

Article No. 2

His Majesty the King of Ava renounces all claims upon, and will abstain from all future interference with the principality of Assam and its dependencies, and also with the contiguous petty States of Cachar and Jyntea.

With regard to Munnipore (Manipur), it is stipulated that, should Gumbheer Singh desire to return to that country, he shall be recognised by the King of Ava as Rajah thereof.

(Signed Archibald Campbell) (L.S.)
Largeen Meonja,
(Woonghee)
(Signed) T.C. Robertson
Captain Royal Navy (L.S)
(Signed Hy. D. Chads
Captain Royal Navy (L.S.)

(Seal of the lotoo)
Shwagum Woon
Atawoon

APPENDIX-V

The Manipur Merger Agreement 1949

Agreement made on this twenty-first day of September 1949 between the Governor General of India and His Highness the Maharajah of Manipur.

Whereas in the best interests of the State of Manipur as well as of the Dominion of India it is desirable to provide for the administration of the said State by or under the authority of the Dominion Government.

It is hereby agreed as follows:

Article No. 1

His Highness the Maharaja of Manipur hereby cedes to the Dominion Government full and exclusive authority, jurisdiction and powers for and in relation to the governance of the State to the Dominion Government on the fifteenth day of October 1949 (hereinafter referred to as 'the said day')

As from the said day the Dominion Government will be competent to exercise the said powers, authority and jurisdiction in such manner and through such agency as it may think fit.

Article No. 2

His Highness the Maharaja shall continue to enjoy the same personal rights, privileges, dignities, titles, authority over religious observances, customs, usages, rites and ceremonies and institutions in charge of the same in the State, which he would have enjoyed had this agreement not been made.

Article No. 3

His Highness the Maharaja shall with effect from the said day be entitled to receive for his life-time from the revenues of the State annually for his privy purse the sum of Rupees three lakhs free of all taxes.

This amount is intended to cover all the expenses of the Ruler and his family, including expenses on account of his personal staff and armed guards, maintenance of his residences, marriages and other ceremonies, etc., and the allowances to the Ruler's relations who on the date of execution of this agreement were in receipt of such allowances from the revenues of the States, and will neither be increased nor reduced for any reason whatsoever.

The Government of India undertake that the said sum of Rupees three lakhs shall be paid to His Highness the Maharaja in four equal instalments in advance at the beginning of each quarter from the State treasury or at such other treasury as may be specified by the Government of India.

Article No. 4

His Highness the Maharaja shall be entitled to the full ownership, use and enjoyment of all private properties (as distinct from State properties) belonging to him on the date of this agreement. His Highness the Maharaja will furnish to the Dominion Government before the first January 1950 an inventory of all the immovable property, securities and cash balance held by him as such private property.

If any dispute arises as to whether any item of property is the private property of His Highness the Maharaja or State property, it shall be referred to a judicial officer qualified to be appointed as a High Court Judge, and the decision of that officer shall be final and binding on both parties:

Provided that His Highness the Maharaja's right to the use of the residence known as 'Redlands' and 'Les Chatalettes' in Shillong, and the property in the town of Gauhati known as 'Manipuri Basti' shall not be questioned.

Article No. 5

All the members of His Highness's family shall be entitled to all the personal rights, privileges, dignities and titles enjoyed by them whether within or outside the territories of the State, immediately before the 15th August, 1947.

Article No. 6

The Dominion Government guarantees the succession, according to law and custom, to the *gaddi* (throne) of the State and to His Highness, the Maharaja's personal rights, privileges, dignities, titles, authority over religious observances, customs, usages, rites and ceremonies and institutions in charge of the same in the State.

Article No. 7

No enquiry shall be made by or under the authority of the Government of India, and no proceedings shall lie in any Court in Manipur, against His Highness the Maharaja whether in a personal capacity or otherwise in respect of anything done or omitted to be done by him or under his authority during the period of his administration of that State.

Article No. 8

1. The Government of India hereby guarantees either the continuance in service of the permanent members or the Public Services of Manipur on conditions which will be not less advantageous than those on which they were serving before the date on which the administration of

Manipur is made over to the Government of India or the payment of reasonable compensation.

2. The Government of India further guarantees the continuance of pensions and leave salaries sanctioned by His Highness the Maharaja to the servants of the State who have retired or proceeded on leave preparatory to retirement, before the date on which the Administration of Manipur is made over to the Government of India.
3. The Government of India undertake to make suitable provisions for the employment of Manipuris in the various branches of Public Services, and in every way encourage Manipuris to join them. They also undertake to preserve various laws, customs and conventions prevailing in the State pertaining to the social, economic and religious life of the people.

Article No. 9

Except with the previous sanction of the Government of India no proceedings, civil or criminal, shall be instituted against any person in respect of any act done or purporting to be done in the execution of his duties as a servant of the State before the day on which the administration is made over to the Government of India.

In confirmation whereof Mr. Vapal Pangunni Menon, Advisor to the Government of India in the Ministry of States, has appended his signature on behalf and with the authority of the Governor General of India and His Highness Maharaja Bodhchandra Singh, Maharaja of Manipur has appended his signature on behalf of himself, his heirs and successors.

Bodhchandra Singh,
Maharaja of Manipur
V.P. Menon
Advisor to the Government of India,
Ministry of States

Sri Prakasa
Governor of Assam, Shillong
September 21, 1949

Bibliography

Primary Sources

Constitutional Documents

Constitutional Assembly Debates (1947-49).
The Government of India Act, 1919.
The Government of India Act, 1935.
The Manipur Constitutional Legislative Act, 1947.
The Draft Constitution of India, 1949.
The Present Constitution of India.
Proceedings of Parliamentary Debates (1967-1970), New Delhi.
The Government of Union Territories Act, 1963.
The North-East Reorganisation Act, 1971.
The Manipur University Act, 1980.

Interview

Interview with Shri I. Tompok Singh, M.L.A. Ex. Home Minister, Manipur Legislative Assembly on 20 January, 1990.

Interview with Md. Helaluddin, M.L.A., Ex Cabinet Minister, Manipur Legislative Assembly on 2 May 1990.

Interview with Dr. Nimaichand Luwang, M.L.A., Ex State Minister, Manipur Legislative Assembly on 31 May 1990.

Interview with Dr. H. Borbabu Singh, Speaker, Manipur Legislative Assembly on 3 July 1990.

The Report of the Administration, Government of Manipur, Imphal, 1973-1990.

The Report of the Annual Administration, Tribal Development Department, Manipur, Imphal, 1983-1984, and 1984-1985.

Secondary Sources

Books

Aiyar, S.P. and Mehta, Usha (ed): *Essays in Indian Federation*, Allied Publishers P. Ltd., Bombay, 1965.

Alexandrowiez, C.H.: *Constitutional Development in India*, Oxford University Press, London, 1957.

Ashok Chandra: *Indian Administration*, George Allen and Unwin Ltd., 2nd Edition, London, 1967.

Ashok Chandra: *Federalism in India*, George Allen and Unwin Ltd., London, 1965.

Austin Graville: *The Indian Constitution: Cornerstone of A Nation*, Oxford University Press, London, 1966.

Banerjee Anil Chandra (ed): *Indian Constitutional Documents*, Vol. 1, 2nd Edn., A Mukherjee & Co. Pvt. Ltd., Calcutta, 1948.

Basu, D.D.: *Commentary on the Constitution of India*, S.C. Sarkar & Sons (P) Ltd., Calcutta, 1954 and 1967.

Bhattacharjee Arun: *History of Ancient India*, Sterling Publishers, New Delhi, 1st Edn., 1979.

Bombwall K.R.: *National Power and State Autonomy*, Meenakshi Publication, Meerut, 1977.

Dahiya, N.S.: *Office of the Government in India*, Sundeep Prakashan, New Delhi, 1979.

Dayal, S.: *The Constitutional Law of India*, Law Agency, Allahabad, 1971.

Dhavan Rajiv (Dr): *President's Rule in India*, N.M. Tripathi Pvt. Ltd., Bombay, 1979.

Dicey, A.V.: *Law of Constitution*, Macmillan & Co. Ltd., 10th Edn., London, 1960.

Dongerkery, S.R.: *University Autonomy in India*, Lelvani Publishing House, Bombay, 1967.

Durga Das: *India from Curzon to Nehru and After*, Collins St. James Place, London, 1969.

Encyclopaedia Britanica: *Encyclopaedia Britenica*, Vol. 10, Inc, William Benton Publisher, USA, 1971 Edn.

Gajendragadkar P.B.: *The Constitution of India: Its Philosophy and Basic Postulates*, Oxford University, Press, Bombay, 1969.

Gehlot N.S.: *State Governors in India: Trends and Issues*, Gitanjali Publishing House, New Delhi, 1985.

Gehlot N.S.: *The Office of the Governor: Its Constitutional Image and Reality*, Chugh Publication, Allahabad, 1977.

Goyal O.P.: *India Government and Politics*, Life and Light Publishers, New Delhi, 1979.

Gupta M.G. (ed): *Aspects of Indian Constitution*, Central Book Depot, Allahabad, 1956.

Haqqi, S.A.H. (ed): *Union-State Relation in India*, Meenakshi, Meerut, 1967.

Iqbal Narain: *State Politics in India*, Meenakshi Prakashan, Meerut, 1967.

Iyengar, T.S.: *Centre-State Relations in India*, University of Mysore, Mysore, 1975.

Jain, M.P.: *Indian Constitutional Law*, N.M. Tripathi, Pvt. Ltd., Bombay, 1972.

Jacdei Alice: *Constitutional Development since Independence*, N.M. Tripathi, Pvt. Ltd., Bombay 1975.

Jennings Sir Ivor: *The British Constitution*, Cambridge University Press Cambridge, 1968.

Jennings Sir Ivor: *Some Characteristics of the Indian Constitution*, Oxford University Press London, 1953.

Keith, A.B.: *A Constitutional History of India*, Central Book Depot, Allahabad, 2nd Edn., 1961.

Khanna and Chopra: *India Ancient and Medieval*, The Macmillan Company of India Ltd., Delhi, 1976.

Ksh. Bimola Devi: *Government and Politics in Manipur 1950-1980*, An unpublished thesis submitted for the Degree of Ph.D., Gauhati University, 1980.

Lal, A.B. (ed): *The Indian Parliament*, Chaitanya Publishing House, Allahabad, 1955.

Laski, Harold J: *Parliamentary Government in England: A Commentary*, George Allen & Unwin Ltd., London, 7th Edn., 1967.

Mukherjee Panchananda (ed): *Indian Constitutional Documents*, Thacker, Spink & Co., Calcutta, 2nd Edn., 1918.

Manshi, K.M.: *Indina Constitutional Documents*, Bhartiya Vidhya Bhavan, Bombay, 1967.

Namboodripad, E.M.S.: *Kerala and the Ugly Face of the Congress*, Communist Party Publication, New Delhi, 1961.

N. Sanajoaba (ed): *Basic Issues on Centre-State Relation*, OM Sons Publication, Gauhati, 1985.

Noorani, A.G.: *India's Constitution and Politics*, Jaico Publishing House, Bombay, 1970.

Pavate D.C.: *My Days as Governor*, Vikas Publishing, New Delhi, 1974.

Rao, K. Subba: *Conflict in Indian Polity*, S. Chand, New Delhi, 1970.

Sahgal, Nayantara: *Indira Gandhi's Emergency and Style*, Vikas Publishing House, New Delhi, 1978.

Sahni Sati (ed): *Centre-State Relations*, Vikas Publishers, New Delhi, 1984.

Saheray, H.K.: *A Legal Study of Constitutional Development of India*, Navbharat Publishers, Calcutta, 1970.

Sankhdher, M.M. (ed): *Framework of the Indian Politics*, Gitanjali Publishers, New Delhi, 1983.

Santharam, K.: *Union-State Relations in India*, Asia Publishing House, Bombay, 1963.

Sarkar Jadunath: *History of Aurangzeb*, Vol. I, Orient Longman Ltd., New Delhi, 1972.

Sen, D.K.: *A Comparative Study of the Indian Constitution*, Orient Longman, Calcutta, 1960.

Seervai, H.M.: *Constitutional Law of India: A Critical Commentary*, N.M. Tripathi Pvt. Ltd., Bombay, 1967.

Shakespear, L.W.: *History of Assam Rifles*, St. Mertines Street, Macmillan & Co. Ltd., London, 1929.

Sharma, S.R.: *Mughal Empire in India*, Lashim Narayan Agrawal Educational Publishers, Agra-3, 1979.

Sharma, Shri Ram: *Now India is Governed*, Central Book Depot, Allahabad, 1954.

Sharma, B.M.: *The Republic of India*, Asia Publishing House, Bombay, 1966.

Shiva Rao, B.: *The Framing of the Indian Constitution*, The Indian Institute of Public Administration, New Delhi, 1967.

Shukla, V.N.: *The Constitution of India*, Eastern Book Co., Lucknow, 1970.

Shrinivasan, N.: *Democratic Government in India*, World Press, Calcutta, 1954.

Sikri, S.L.: *The Constitutional History of India*, Vol. I, S. Nagin & Co., Jullandar, 1964.

Singh, G.N.: *Landmarks in Indian Constitutional and National Movement 1600-1919*. Vol. I, Atma Ram & Sons, New Delhi, 1952.

Singh, G.N.: *Role of the Governors in India*, Kitab Mahal Publishers, Allahabad, 1968.

Siwach, J.R.: *Dynamics of the Indian Government and Policy*, Sterling Publishers Pvt. Ltd., New Delhi, 1985.

Siwach, J.R.: *The Office of the Governor: A Critical Study*, Sterling Publishers, Pvt. Ltd., New Delhi, 1977.

Srivastava, Meera (Mrs): *Constitutional Crisis in the States of India*, Concept Publishers, New Delhi, 1980.

Sri Prakasa: *State Governors in India*, Meenakshi Parkashan, Meerut, 1966.

Thomson, Edward and Garrat, G.T: *Rise and Fulfilment of the British Rule in India*, Central Book Depot, Allahabad, 1969.

Wheare, K.C.: *The English Constitution*, Oxford University Press, London, 1963.

Wheare, K.C.: *Modern Constitutions*, Oxford University Press, London, 1963.

Journals, Magazines, Periodicals, etc.

The Journal of African and Asian Studies, Vol. I, No. 2, Delhi, 1968.

The Journal of Constitutional and Parliamentary Studies, Vol. 3, No. 1, January-March, New Delhi, 1969.

The Journal of the Indian Law Institute, Vol. 12, No. 1, January-March, 1970.

The Journal of Political Science Review, Vol. 5, No. 1, January-March, Rajasthan University, Jaipur, 1967.

The Journal of Political Science, Vol. XXII, No. 184, January-December, Delhi University, 1961.

Indian Journal of Public Administration, Vol. XVI, No. 3, July-September, New Delhi, 1970.

The Journal of the Society for Study of State Governments, Vol. IV, Nos. 3 and 4, July-December, Varanasi, 1971.

The Modern Review, Vol. LXXXIV, No. IV, August, Calcutta, 1953.

The Organiser, Vol. 12, New Delhi, 1968.

The Parliamentary Studies, Vol. XV, No. 12, December, New Delhi, 1971.

Swarajya, 10 (34), February 19, Madras, 1966.

Times Weekly, Vol. 3, No. 5, September, 10, New Delhi, 1972.

Eastern Economist, Vol. 52, No. 21, May, New Delhi, 1969.

Articles

Appadorai, A.: "Guidelines for Governors", *Eastern Economist*, Vol. 52, No. 21, May 21, New Delhi, 1969.

Ashok Mitra: "This Government is self destablising itself", *The Telegraph*, dated the 24th August 1988.

Ashok, K.: "Role of the Governor in Emerging Pattern of Centre-State Relations", *Journal of Constitution and Parliamentary Studies*, Vol. 55, No. 3, July-September, New Delhi, 1971.

C.S. Pandit: "With Nurul Kassen in, Raj Bhavan is likely to become open house for Scholars". *Amrita Bazar Patrika*, dated the 20th August, 1986.

Dahiya, M.S.: "Governor's Power to Dismiss the Chief Minister". *The Modern Review*, Vol. CXXVIII, No. 6, June, Calcutta, 1971.

Dole, N.V.: "The Position of the Chancellor Governor in India", *The Journal of Political Science*, Vol. XXII, No. 184, January-December, Delhi University, 1961.

G.C. Shekar: "Governor suggests T.N. Government Dismissal", *The Telegraph*, dated the 30th January, 1988.

Indrajit: "Governors, Politics and Nehru", *Economics Times*, dated 4th November, 1980.

Iqbal Narain: "The Governor—The Problem of Role Identification", *Journal of African and Asian Studies*, Vol. 1, No. 2, Delhi University, 1968.

Joshi K.C.: "The Governor's Power to Dismiss the Ministry", *Journal of the Indian Law Institute*, Vol. 12, No. 1, January-March, New Delhi, 1970.

K.R. Sundar Rajan: "Constitution or Football?" *Amrita Bazar Patrika*, dated the 12th May, 1987.

M.A. Hafiz: "Opposition forces Governor to have U.P. Assembly", *Amrita Bazar Patrika*, the 3rd March, 1987.

Madhu Limayi: The Anti Defection Law", *Telegraph*, dated the 28th August, 1990.

Nermalendu Bikash Rakshit: "Governor's Veto Power", *Amrita Bazar Patrika*, dated the 16th June, 1986.

Pitambar Das: "The Governor is not bound to accept the Chief Minister's advice to dissolve the House", *The Organiser*, 22(20), 28 December, New Delhi, 1968.

Rao, K.V.: "The Governor in the Constituent Assembly", *The Journal of the Society for Study of State Governments*', Vol. IV, No. 3-4, July-Dec., Varanasi, 1971.

Rao, N. Rang: "The Governor and the State", *Times Weekly*, Vol. 3, No. 5, September 10, New Delhi, 1972.

Rau, S.K.: "The Governor's Role", *Swarajya*, 10(34), February 19, Madras, 1966.

S. Sahay: "Subversion of th Constitution", *The Telegraph*, dated the 3rd May, 1990.

S. Sahay: "The Dubious role of the Nagaland Governor", *The Telegraph*, dated the 18th August, 1988.

Sarkar, R.C.S.: "The Office of the Governor", *Journal of Constitutional and Parliamentary Studies*, Vol. 3, No. 1, January-March, New Delhi, 1969.

Shubha Singh: "Desam, Governor at Loggerheads", *The Telegraph*, dated the 8th February, 1987.

Sinha, Uraj Mohan: "Governor's Invitation to Form the Government", *Journal of Political Science Review*, Vol. 6, No. 1, January-March, Rajasthan University, Jaipur, 1967.

Srivastava Arun: "The Ordinance Raj in Bihar", *The Amrita Bazar Patrika*, dated the 22nd February, 1987.

Syeed, S.M.: "The Governor—A Titular Head", *Parliamentary Studies*, Vol. XV, No. 12, December, New Delhi, 1971.

Vishnu Sahay: "Governor's Role in Administration", *Indian Journal of Public Administration*, Vol. XVI, No. 3, July-September, New Delhi, 1970.

Wasleir Hussain: "Governor suggests T.N. Government Dismissal", *The Telegraph*, dated the 30th January, 1988.

Yusuf Jameel: "Shah Government Fails on all Fronts", *The Telegraph*, dated the 3rd July, 1985.

News Papers

Amrita Bazar Patrika.

Assam Tribune.

The Hindu.

Hindustan Times.

The Telegraph.

Times of India.

The Statesman.

Local Papers

Ching-Tam (Hill and Valley, in Manipuri).

E-hou (Wave, in Manipuri).

Huiyen Lanpao (Voice of War, in Manipuri).

hollao (Slogan, in Manipuri).

Lalmei-Thanbi, (Lightening of War Fire, in Manipuri).

Matam (Times, in Manipuri).

Poknapham (Birth land, in Manipuri).
Prajatantra (People's view, in Manipuri).
Simanta Patrika (Border Paper, in Manipuri).
Toknga (Rumour, in Manipuri).

Index